F. Frelligh
1705 Cord.
Ft. Wayne, IN 46805

W9-CCT-019

A prayer book
for the later years

FIRE
in the
SOUL

A prayer book
for the later years

FIRE
in the
SOUL

Richard Lyon Morgan

UPPER
ROOM BOOKS™
NASHVILLE

Fire in the Soul: A Prayer Book for the Later Years
Copyright © 2000 by Richard Lyon Morgan
All rights reserved.

No part of this book may be reproduced in any manner whatsoever without written permission of the publisher except in brief quotations embodied in critical articles or reviews. For information, address The Upper Room®, 1908 Grand Avenue, Nashville, Tennessee 37212.

Upper Room® Web address: http://www.upperroom.org

UPPER ROOM®, UPPER ROOM BOOKS™ and design logos are trademarks owned by The Upper Room®, Nashville, Tennessee. All rights reserved.

All scripture quotations unless otherwise noted are from The New Revised Standard Version of the Bible, copyright © 1989 by the Division of Christian Education of the National Council of the Churches of Christ in the United States of America. Used by permission.

Scripture excerpt marked NAB is taken from the *New American Bible,* copyright © 1970 Confraternity of Christian Doctrine, Inc., Washington, DC. Used with permission. All rights reserved. No part of the New American Bible may be reproduced by any means without permission in writing from the copyright owner.

Scripture quotations designated KJV are from the King James Version of the Bible.

Scripture quotations identified as NIV are from the *Holy Bible, New International Version.* Copyright © 1973, 1978, 1984 International Bible Society. Used by permission of Zondervan Bible Publishers.

The publisher gratefully acknowledges permission to reproduce the copyrighted material appearing in this book. Credit lines for this material appear in the Notes and Permissions Section which begins on page 155.

Cover Design: Jim Bateman
Cover Photograph: Byron Jorjorian
First Printing: 2000

The Library of Congress Cataloging-in-Publication Data

Morgan, Richard Lyon, 1929–
       Fire in the soul: a prayer book for the later years / Richard L.
   Morgan.
         p.   cm.
      ISBN 0-8358-0879-3
      1. Aged—Prayer-books and devotions—English.   I. Title.
   BV4580.M569 2000
   242'.85—dc21   99-34605
                                                                                CIP

Printed in the United States of America

In memory of my mother,
Margaret Lyon Morgan (1901–1967),
who first taught me to pray,
and whose life was a prayer for her children.
Her death was an answer to our prayers
that God would send angels to take her home.

Other Books by Richard Lyon Morgan

Graceful Aging: Sermons for Third Agers

Is There Life after Divorce in the Church?

No Wrinkles on the Soul:
A Book of Readings for Older Adults

I Never Found That Rocking Chair:
God's Call at Retirement

From Grim to Green Pastures:
Meditations for the Sick and Their Caregivers

Autumn Wisdom: A Book of Readings

Remembering Your Story:
A Guide to Spiritual Autobiography

With Faces to the Evening Sun:
Faith Stories from the Nursing Home

Contents

My life is an instant
An hour which passes by;
My life is a moment
Which I have no power to stay.
You know, O my God,
That to love you here on earth
I have only today.

—*Thérèse of Lisieux, 1873–1897*

FOREWORD

Fire in the Soul: A Prayer Book for the Later Years arrived on my desk for review at a time when I was experiencing a particularly severe "dark night of the soul" regarding my own aging and the aging of society in general. My struggle for faith in the context of physical decline had come to a peak very suddenly. Within the course of the previous week two older women friends had died lonely and emotionally unresolved deaths. In addition, three of my aged patients—all without advance directives—had been placed in long-term care facilities, to be kept barely alive on life-support technology. Just one—the only "success" of the week—made it into a hospice program. I was feeling like a total failure as a health-care provider and as a friend. In addition, I was struggling with my own aging, asking myself, "How will I end up—a childless woman with no living relatives and a husband whose own father died suddenly at forty-four? Who will take care of me if Ron dies before I do?" The darkest realization was that if I survive my husband there is no one who is required to bury me! These were heavy ruminations, very unlike my usual optimism about life in the later—and frailer—years.

The following afternoon Ron and I went to the funeral home to attend the wake of one of the women. To my great grief we were the only mourners present. I was devastated that a life could come to such a level of disconnection from the human community. I wondered darkly if anyone would bother coming to the funeral home to visit me when I die. The question haunted me throughout the rest of the day and into the evening. My sleep was fitful and ended at 3:00 a.m. Unable to sleep or even relax, I told myself, "You might as well get up and do something useful. Read Dick Morgan's book and start writing the foreword for it." What an incredible blessing this middle-of-the-night decision was. (Perhaps my faithful old guardian angel, Paula, nudged me out of my disturbing thoughts to provide me with the solace of this prayer book.) It is just what I—at fifty-two—needed. And it will continue to be just what I need if I make it to one hundred two!

Fire in the Soul is based on Richard Morgan's belief that "In a person's later years, the life of prayer is not a luxury; it is an imperative priority . . . the one thing necessary," a belief affirmed by his own experience of having lived seventy years. His reflection on his own and others' aging process is the source of his strong conviction that we face seven major developmental tasks as we progress from being "young old" to "mature old" to the "oldest old." These tasks range from discovering God's call at retirement, to redeeming our suffering during times of frailty

and pain, to finally facing our losses and the nearness of death. The honest and potent prayers—his own and others—"fit" each of these tasks to perfection.

Fire in the Soul promises to help any reader reflect on personal aging as well as the aging of loved ones, clients, patients, parishioners, and the aging of our global society. It is not necessary that the reader be experiencing a particular stage of development to appreciate the prayers in all of the stages. For me on that dark night, reading the entire book from cover to cover was what I needed for my own spiritual nurture. Each and every prayer offered me a new and different glimmer of hope for my own aging— and for the aging of those in my care. I am firmly convinced that it is only when we who provide service to the elderly honestly encounter our own fears of aging that we can face those in the young-old, mature-old, and oldest-old categories with a new-found understanding of the meaning of late life.

For the older adult, each prayer corresponds to a real-life spiritual need. There is no white-washing of the challenging nature of spiritual tasks of later life in this work; Richard Morgan "tells it as it is" through his honesty with God in these prayers. He deals directly with the need to let go of grudges to the need to deal with the fact that one did not live up to his or her life potential. As he does in *With Faces to the Evening Sun*, his wonderful, life-giving book of poignant faith stories in the nursing home, Richard Morgan

presents practical scenarios and offers simple but profound lessons. I especially appreciate the honesty with which he presents his own struggles.

Fire in the Soul is a sourcebook of prayers and reflection for a variety of occasions and for many different kinds of users: older adults themselves, those ministering to older adults, and those just beginning to grapple with the reality of aging—all of us who desire to become emblazoned with the fire of God's blessing of one hundred twenty years.

Jane Marie Thibault, Ph.D.
Clinical Gerontologist
Associate Professor of Family and Community Medicine
School of Medicine, University of Louisville (Kentucky)

Preface

In a person's later years, the life of prayer is not a luxury—it is an imperative priority. Freed from the demands of family and work, we now have precious opportunities to move from "many things" to "the one thing necessary." Gandhi called prayer the key of the morning and the bolt of the evening. Prayer unlocks doors of new opportunities. When Peter prayed at Caesarea, men from Cornelius stopped at his house and God opened a door for the Gentiles to be welcomed into the Christian church. Prayer is also a lock for the night. As the ancient psalmist prayed, "I will both lie down and sleep in peace; for you alone, O LORD, make me lie down in safety" (Ps. 4:8).

This prayer book is not to be read once and put away. It is intended as a constant guide for your spiritual life. You can open it at random or select readings by theme or section. You can keep it by your bedside and read a prayer to end the day, or keep it on the coffee- or kitchen table in your home to have available at any time. You will find treasured prayers of saints through the ages that we can make our own. The timelessness of these prayers makes this volume a continuing and valued resource.

I wrote these prayers in the years following my "retirement" and tried to relate them to my own spiritual journey. They speak not only to my needs as an older person but also to countless others in the third and fourth ages of life. Also, these prayers can be guidelines for younger generations who seek a spiritual understanding of the later years.

I have reached the magical age of seventy. As I reflect on the journey we call aging, I find that seven major tasks confront us in our later years. These prayers seek God's help as we meet these late-life challenges.

Two major tasks face the *young old:* (1) discovering God's call at retirement, and (2) moving to deeper contemplation. When a person's full-time work ends, a new vocation can begin. God continues to call us as long as we live. The earlier years of late life are a time for us deepen the inner life. All too often the temptation is to wallpaper the empty spaces with busy activities. But soul work—cultivating a contemplative life with God—is a never-ending challenge.

The *mature old* face three tasks: (1) accepting our aging, (2) discerning the meaning of our stories, and (3) mentoring the next generations. When we first retire we try to deny our aging. Most of us want to live to a ripe old age, especially when we consider the alternative. We want to live long, but we don't want to get old. Captivated by the cult of youth, we'll do anything to deny that we are getting old. But as we do age, we discover that youth doesn't have a monopoly on excitement,

beauty, and achievement. We realize that the later years have their own unique value. As we begin to experience some of the inevitable issues of growing older, we come to accept our aging.

Remembering the past is a way in which we can affirm our identity and the value of our own life story as we grow older. Claiming our stories—with their celebrations and crises—can bring a sense of integrity to our later years. The wisdom of older persons needs to be shared in a mentoring role with the next generations. We need to tell our own stories to younger generations so this valued wisdom will not be lost.

For the *oldest old*, two challenges remain: (1) facing loss and death, and (2) redeeming our suffering. The crippling experience of a shrinking circle of friends, the loss of independence, and constant threats to health make us aware of our own mortality. We need to learn how to accept these losses and face our own death with courage and hope. As one lives longer and longer, physical decline, if not major assaults on the body, will occur. Depression may ensue, unless this suffering is transformed by a heroic spirit and a sense of humor.

This *Prayer Book for the Later Years* addresses these major tasks. It is all too easy to give up hope and to despair as the later years bring their inevitable issues. Prayer bridges the gap between us and God.

Nor is this book only for those in their later years. During our middle years we make financial preparation for retirement. We should also be

building our *spiritual income* for old age. This book can provide that spiritual income for those anticipating the later years.

In "Prayer Is the Soul's Sincere Desire," hymn writer James Montgomery said it well: "[Prayer] is the motion of a hidden fire that trembles in the breast." All through history, God had kindled the flame of sacred love in the hearts of people. The ancient Levites received the command, "The fire on the altar shall be kept burning; it shall not go out" (Lev. 6:12). Moses witnessed Yahweh's awesome presence in the burning bush (Exod. 3:2) and led the Israelites out of bondage by a pillar of fire. Two disciples, walking on the road to Emmaus on that first Easter afternoon, had given up hope. But they were joined by a stranger whose presence caused their hearts to burn with hope and joy (Luke 24:32). Fire symbolizes the gift of the Spirit at Pentecost (Acts 2:3).

Blaise Pascal had an experience of God's presence in 1654, which he described as "fire." He sewed the words of his prayer into the lining of his jacket next to his heart, where it was found at his death. At a society in Aldersgate Street where he heard read Luther's preface to the Epistle to the Romans, John Wesley felt his heart strangely warmed, and the evangelical revival followed. Catherine of Siena knew the fire. She wrote,

> Your fire surpasses all fire, because your
> fire alone burns without destroying.
> The flames of your fire reach into the

soul. . . . But far from damaging the
soul, your fire sets it ablaze with love.[1]

In the later years, as the passion and ardor of
youth wanes and as the warmth of summer fades
into the shadows of autumn, we must seek to
discover this sacred fire of faith through prayer.

As you meditate on these prayers, may these
words of Charles Wesley become your own:

O Thou who camest from above,
The pure celestial fire to impart,
Kindle a flame of sacred love
Upon the mean altar of my heart!

There let it for thy glory burn
with inextinguishable blaze,
and trembling to its source return,
in humble prayer and fervent praise.

Jesus, confirm my heart's desire
to work and speak and think for thee;
Still let me guard the holy fire,
And still stir up thy gift in me.

[1]*Book of Prayers*, compiled by Robert Van de Weyer (New York: HarperCollins, 1993), 88.

For a Christian in old age
only one thing can be at the
core of life—prayer.

—*Romano Guardini*

I.

DISCERNING GOD'S CALL
AT RETIREMENT

*Not that I have already obtained this, or have
already reached the goal. . . . But this one thing
I do: forgetting what lies behind and
straining forward to what lies ahead, I press
on toward the goal for the prize of the heavenly
call of God in Christ Jesus.*

—Philippians 3:12–14

AT RETIREMENT

You love me, eternal God, when I leave the world of work and lose the identity I acquired through years of labor. Keep me sensitive to your will for me now. Remind me of Abraham and Sarah, Anna and Simeon, to whom your call came later in life. Give me grace to enjoy my new freedom, to cherish my leisure time, and to care for others. Above all, help me not to rush about, or rust out, but to rest in you. Amen.

FOR COURAGE AND GRATITUDE

Lord God of Israel, how much I admire Caleb. At eighty-five he was not content to settle down to an easy life in Canaan, or to be put out to pasture, but was ready to fight for the land promised him. I need his spirit in these early days of retirement, when all I think about are my entitlements and benefits. Help me to realize that even as I accept these gifts I have earned, I owe much to your grace, which is unearned. Amen.

FOR DISCERNMENT

Grant me, O Lord, to know what is
worth knowing,
to love what is worth loving,
to praise what delights you most,

to value what is precious in your sight,
to hate what is offensive to you.
Do not let me judge by what I see,
nor pass sentence according to what I
hear,
but to judge rightly between things
that differ,
and above all to search out and to do
what pleases you, through Jesus Christ
our Lord.

—*Thomas à Kempis, 1380–1471*

THOSE EARLY DAYS

Surprising God, I need my second wind in these retirement years. Athletes seem to get it when they have spent themselves. After expending all their energies, just when it seems they have run out of gas, they get that new burst of energy. Well, Lord, I admit I am worn out. The years have taken their toll. I need to press on for your high calling in these retirement years, but I need that second wind of your spirit to carry me beyond my fatigue. Amen.

THERE IS STILL WONDER

Ancient of Days, even this new freedom is too short for me to appreciate all the wonders of your world. I now have more time for reflection

and contemplation. Grant me a holy curiosity about life. Help me never to feel that life is over and all that is left is a rocking chair on the porch. Give me grace to explore new scenes, revisit old memories. Show me each day the miracle of the moment, and direct my footsteps to quiet libraries, still waters, and the laughter of children. Amen.

WHEN THE HONEYMOON ENDS

Dear Lord, the first exciting days of retirement are gone, and now the reality has hit home. It was nice to do nothing for awhile. It felt like playing hooky from school. I laughed when they handcuffed me at my retirement party and gave me the keys. What doors do they open? Or do they keep me locked to the past? I know my life is not over. But the honeymoon has ended. I long to know what is next in this puzzling journey. Help me to trust when I cannot see. Amen.

AMPLIUS

(A Poem That Becomes a Prayer)
I must make my way to the mountains,
   and find
a path to the sea,
let the far and silent places become a
   part of me,
for my world has grown so small, that

there is no room at all
for my spirit twisting, turning to be
    free.

I must dwell awhile in the desert or
    walk beside a lake,
for something asleep within me is
    trying to come awake,
and my life has dwindled down to a
    single, little town
and my spirit is twisting, turning to be
    free.

I will go beyond horizon, trace a
    western star,
rest my eyes on a prairie reaching wide
    and far.
For this journey, I have no guide save what
seems inside, where
my spirit is twisting, turning to be free.

I may come once more to freedom in
    this same,
familiar street,
break out of the bondage if I really
    meet
those who, knowing me, have eyes
    with which to see,
my spirit twisting, turning to be free.

—*John David Burton*

WHEN TIME STANDS STILL

Gracious God, for many weeks it was nice to wake up in the morning, laugh at the alarm clock, and set my own schedule. I had a leisurely breakfast, watched the birds at my feeder, and was just plain lazy. The day was like that. And at evening I sat on the deck and watched the sunset until the stars appeared. It was great. But now, months later, every day seems the same. I'm by myself a lot, and have simply run out of things to do. I've rearranged my scrapbooks, watched old reruns, and played with my computer. God, I'm tired of this free time. I had hoped that retirement would be different—exciting new adventures, travel. I guess I read too many ads in retirement magazines that promised the moon. Now reality has set in. I know I shouldn't complain, but I can tell you how I feel. I promise not to whine or recline, but I need to do a lot of work on myself so I can hear your voice calling me to new directions. Amen.

BUSYNESS

God My Help Now, it seems so incongruous that I feel more rushed and pulled in different directions than I ever did before I retired. At times it feels good to be busy, when I swing into action and check off my daily "to do's" list. I pride myself that I am not really retired. And yet being busy is not what you want for me. I need time to

reflect, to be with you, to be with myself, to be with others. When my calendar is so clocked full of activities, I get out of whack. Teach me to be active, but not busy. Help me to balance quiet with service. May these years find me growing in grace, not just doing more things. Amen.

A BUSY, FRANTIC LIFE

How is it, my God, that you have given me this hectic busy life when I have so little time to enjoy your presence. Throughout the day people are waiting to speak with me, and even at meals I have to continue talking to people about their needs and problems. During sleep itself I am still thinking and dreaming about the multitude of concerns that surround me. I do all this not for own sake, but for yours. To me my present pattern of life is a torment; I only hope that for you it is truly a sacrifice of love. I know that you are constantly beside me, yet I am usually so busy that I ignore you. If you want me to remain so busy, please force me to think about and love you even in the midst of such hectic activity. If you do not want me so busy, please release me from it, showing how others can take over my responsibilities.

—*Teresa of Avila, 1515–1582*

A PRAYER FOR KAIROS TIME

It has been a difficult time, bountiful God, since the first exciting days of retirement ended. At first I went around as if in a daze, so thankful for this new time for myself. Now I feel marooned in a barren wilderness, with no clue as to where I go from here. Time seems to drag on, even more so than when I was working. I am so accustomed to clock time, with neatly lined blocks of my carefully pocketed day-timer, that I don't know how to handle this change. So I wait for your *kairos* time, when all these jagged pieces will fall into place and I will see clearly your will for me in this new time of my life. As you sent Jesus in the fullness of *kairos* time, help me to find my *kairos* time as well. Amen.

EVERYONE'S PRAYER

I lift up my heart, O God, for all who are the prey of anxious fears, who cannot get their minds off themselves and for whom every demand made on them fills them with foreboding, and with the feeling they cannot cope with what is required of them.

Give them the comfort of knowing that this feeling is illness, not cowardice; that millions have felt as they feel, that there is a way through this dark valley, and light at the end of it.

Lead them to those who can help them and understand them and show them the pathway to health and happiness. Comfort and sustain them by the loving presence of the Saviour who knows and understands all our woe and fear, and give them enough courage to face each day, and rest their minds in the thought that thou wilt see them through.

—Charles Wesley, 1707–1788

SPINNING TOPS

How strange—
we are all so ardent in our piety
so careful not to slip up
so intent on making our individual lives
count in the scheme of things
tyrannized by overful diaries
driven by the echo of our 'well done.'
And where does it all lead?

Spinning round like tops
we spiral down before You
in now grubby, tattered clothes
Out of breath.

Deal gently with us, Lord.

—Kathy Keay

THE TOUCH OF THE MASTER'S HAND

Oh Master, we are like an old violin. We used to play a great tune, but now we seem old and frail, marred by life. At times we feel useless, of little worth anymore because we are out of the limelight and forced to play cameo roles. But the music is still there!

Oh Master, take the strings of our lives and make them vibrate once more. Some may want to discard us as old concertos, but your touch can resurrect our music. Some may want to relegate us to the museum of life, but your touch can send new music from the strings of our hearts. Amen.

A PRAYER FROM THE AIR

Lord of heavens, my one true pilot, sitting here in this airplane as we descend to the ground reminds of me these retirement years. The power has been cut, the pitch of the droning engines has changed, and the nose dips, and I know that the flight will soon end. There has come a definitive moment, a feeling signaling that the rush of life has ended, and I am moving into the final phase of my existence. As in the case of the plane's descent, nothing has really changed but things have begun to wind down around me. I am clearing out some of the clutter in my life, thinning out some activities and beginning to take seriously the mystery of death and dying.

So, even as the psalmist prayed, "If I take the wings of the morning, and settle at the farthest limits of the sea, even there your hand shall lead me and your right hand shall hold me fast" (Ps. 139:9-10). I put my trust in your hands, knowing you will guide me home. Amen.

AT NIGHT

O Lord God, who has given us the night for rest, I pray that in my sleep my soul may remain awake to you, steadfastly adhering to your love. As I lay aside my cares to relax and relieve my mind, may I not forget your infinite and unresting care for me. And in this way, let my conscience be at peace, that when I rise tomorrow, I am refreshed in body, mind and soul.

—John Calvin, 1509–1564

FOR EXTENDED LIFE

Loving Creator, medical science has indeed extended our years and we are grateful, yet we wonder what this means. We know that being seventy or eighty is nothing strange in these days, but just another stage of life with its opportunities and possibilities. We need to approach these bonus years with endless gratitude for this gift of more time to live. Even when these years

bring inevitable loss and decline, grant us grace to bear these years with courage and hope. Through Jesus Christ our Lord. Amen.

NOT JUST A LONGER LIFE

Lord, despite our extended years, as we enter a new century with even greater possibilities of reaching 120 years of age, there is a lurking, haunting fear that length of days cannot satisfy the hunger of our souls. We have the means to live longer, but do we have any meaning to live for? Will we fulfill the words of the writer, "Remember your creator in the days of your youth, before the days of trouble come, and the years draw near when you will say, 'I have no pleasure in them'" (Eccles. 12:1)? Will these extended years bring sadness and suffering, regret and ruin? Or will we live fully to the end of our days, lost in wonder, love, and praise? Amen.

GOD OF SURPRISES

God of surprises, when I think that being old is a drag on my life, you surprise me in the love of family and friends who nurture me by their attention. God of surprises, just when I am ready to believe I am useless and of little worth anymore, the mailman brings a good word, the telephone rings and someone wants me to help.

God of surprises you are ever with us, just as you surprised those two on the Emmaus road, who thought you were a stranger. As our days go by and our strength weakens, keep surprising us. When our patience fails and life seems dull, keep surprising us . . . until that day when we leave this world and receive the greatest surprise of all! Amen.

GOD CALLS AGAIN

Dear Lord, it seems that all through life you keep asking us to listen for your call, and now as we put down one call, we pick up another. We thank you for the "call" that comes in the later years, as surely as you called Abraham at age seventy-five. It is a call to new beginnings, a seemingly endless journey of faith. Help us to reinvent who we are and what we are to do as ongoing servants of the God who is always calling us. We know that when we retire we feel disconnected from the power and status of our working life. We also miss our work companions. Now they are gone with only lingering memories. Help us not to waste our time, but to fill it as we enjoy you, our neighbors, and the world around us. Help us ever to "press on toward the goal for the prize of the heavenly call of God in Christ Jesus" (Phil. 3:14). Amen.

PRAYER OF A SAINT

Teach us, good Lord,
   to serve you as you deserve;
   to give and not to count the cost;
   to fight and not to heed the wounds;
   to toil and not to seek for rest;
   to labor and not to ask for any reward,
   except that of knowing that we do your will;
through Jesus Christ our Lord. Amen.

—Saint Ignatius of Loyola, 1491–1556

TEN YEARS LATER

Lord, it is ten years since I "retired" and faced
this unknown journey with much fear and
trembling. I know my friends told me that
retirement is when work no longer interferes
with life, but I scarcely believed that. Now, I do.
It has been ten good years of new directions,
renewed energy, and exciting adventures. I
really do have the new freedom to be who I am
and not what the work role demands. I have
the joy of finding ways to serve others and
repay my debt to the world. And most of all I
am myself . . . at last! Amen.

NEW BEGINNINGS

This time of retirement can be a new beginning, O Lord of the Journey. On the first day of time you began your mighty act of creation by calling life out of nothing. On the first day of the week you called Jesus from the tomb and the world began again. This is the first day of the rest of my life. Help me to live as one for whom life is not ending, like a door slammed in my face; but as one for whom life is beginning, as a door opening before me. Give me grace to forget what is behind and to press on to what lies ahead. Amen.

THE PEACE ONLY YOU GIVE

You are not found, O mysterious God, in the shattering noise of the earthquake, or in the raging fire, or in the blustery winds of nature, but in the still, small voice. Why am I so preoccupied with being busy? I confess I am still a slave to the work ethic, each day measured by what I do. But I *am* saved by grace, not by works. I am liberated from clocks and calendars, with precious time for my soul. But I still want to be in the thick of things, and so I fail to find your presence in the thickets of life. All you really ask is that I *be* someone. Help me in these autumn days to find that creative balance between vital involvement and quiet rest. May Christ say to me, "Come unto me, all ye that labor and are heavy laden, and I will give you rest" (Matt. 11:28, KJV). Amen.

II.

MOVING TO DEEPER CONTEMPLATION

I pray that, according to the riches of his glory, he may grant that you be strengthened in your inner being with power through his Spirit.

—Ephesians 3:16

LORD, TEACH US TO PRAY

Lord, I know one thing: I need to pray as I grow older. Sometimes I feel it is because I know my mortality and there has to be something beyond this time and space, more than my life here. Even though prayer has always been an integral part of my life, my need to pray becomes more ingrained with every passing day. As an older person I can relate to the cry of the disciple, "Lord, teach us to pray" (Luke 11:1). Amen.

PRESERVE MY SOUL

Eternal and most glorious God, suffer me not so to undervalue myself as to give away my soul, Thy soul, Thy dear and precious soul, for nothing; and all the world is nothing, if the soul must be given for it. Preserve therefore, my soul, O Lord, because it belongs to Thee, and preserve my body because it belongs to my soul. Thou alone dost steer my boat through all its voyage, but hast a more especial care of it, when it comes to a narrow current, or to a dangerous fall of waters. Thou hast a care of the preservation of my body in all the way of my life; but, in the straits of death, open Thine eyes wider, and enlarge Thy Providence toward me so far that no illness or agony may shake and benumb my soul. Do Thou make my bed in all my sickness that, being used to Thy hand, I may be content with any bed of Thy making.

—John Donne, 1571–1631

HELP ME HOE TO THE END OF THE ROW

Lord of harvest, I am in my autumn years and there is a touch of sadness as the warmth of summer departs, the nights become darker, and the leaves begin falling to the ground. Harvest is the good time of life when we should gather in the fruits of a lifetime's experience and enjoy them in old age. To harvest means we have made a difference in the world and still have a contribution to make. I want to be always looking for new places to discover, new friends to meet, new challenges to face. I want to read new books that feed my soul and to reread old books as if for the first time. I want to stay connected to friends and family, reaching out the hand to help and never being a burden to anyone. Grant, oh Lord, that these harvest years may be mellow ones, full of happy memories, bright new experiences, and a realization of our achievements. Lord, I want to stay *alive* as long as I live. Amen.

THE NEED TO BE STILL

Oh, why is it that we can't seem to find that quiet centeredness that alone saves us from distress? We find it impossible to be still, even for a few moments. Our lives are swamped by clanging cymbals and chattering magpies. We even deliberately try to create noise to fill the silence. Even in these "retirement years" we are

go-go people, always on the move yet often going nowhere. We glance nervously at our watches, become impatient with delays, and wonder why we feel so empty. Help us to find the still waters. Help us to look inward and find you in the depths of our souls. We know we can't be still. We have places to visit, people to see, things to do. But perfect peace can only be found when our minds are stayed on you. Grant us the strength that only comes from your stillness. Amen.

FOR INNER PEACE

Grant us, O Lord, the blessings of those whose minds are stayed on you, so that we may be kept in perfect peace: a peace which cannot be broken. Let not our minds rest upon any creature, but only in the Creator; not upon goods, things, houses, lands, inventions of vanities or foolish fashions, lest, our peace being broken, we become cross and brittle and given over to envy. From all such deliver us, O God, and grant us your peace.

—*George Fox, 1624–1691*

NOW THAT I AM OLDER

Loving Parent, I am sometimes confused and unsure about all these views of prayer. What I really need is to recapture my childlike faith and the simple way I used to talk with you. You were the voice in darkness to whom I cried, the presence felt even when I was afraid. Help me to be a little child again, to fall on my knees at the foot of my bed and to pray with a childlike heart. Dear God, I do love you and I know I can count on you whatever happens. Amen.

WHY DO WE HIDE FROM YOU?

Loving God, why do we hide from you? Why are we so afraid to hear you coming into our lives? Our parents, Adam and Eve, hid from you in the bushes. We still hide—in the bushes of our busyness and in the shrubbery of our schedules. We cram our lives full and crowd you out. Is it any wonder we are so restless, anxious, afraid? Yet your eternal cry pierces our souls—"Where are you?"—those words that haunt us down the days of distracted games and nights of dreamless sleep. Help us to be still and let your love flood us like a searchlight in a murky fog. Can it be that our foolish fears are illusions, and your love is the one reality? Amen.

MORE OAK TREE TIME

Tender God, when I was working most of my days were structured and jammed like a tightly packed suitcase. I had "carpenter time," building my own world and carving out a name

for myself on the tree of life. I had little time for "oak tree time"—just to be, or to spend precious moments with family and enjoy friends. I know I have more opportunity for "oak tree time" now; but I still cling to "carpenter time," thinking that without projects and productive days I am of little worth. Help me, Lord, to take "oak tree time" to stand and stare at the beauty of your world, or watch the glory of a mountain sunset. Amen.

KEEP US CURIOUS, LORD

Ancient of Days, life is too short for us to appreciate fully the wonders of your world. Help us to see the wonders of nature, especially now that life has slowed down and we can watch winter birds feed, revel in spring flowers popping through the soil, and notice the awesome beauty of a snowy day that blankets the earth. Help us to know that as long as we live, every day brings its own marvels to behold and the opportunity to try things we never dared when we were trapped by the conventions of our culture. Show us each day the wonder in the exuberant laughter of little children, in the witty sayings of older people, and in the courage of those who face death. Amen.

NATIVE AMERICAN PRAYER

O Great Spirit,
  whose breath gives life to the world,
  and whose voice is heard in the soft breeze:
We need your strength and wisdom.
Cause us to walk in beauty. Give us eyes
  ever to behold the red and purple sunset.
Make us wise so that we may understand
  what you have taught us.
Help us learn the lessons you have hidden
  in every leaf and rock.
Make us always ready to come to you
  with clean hands and steady eyes,
so when life fades, like the fading sunset,
  our spirits may come to you without shame.
    Amen.

—Traditional Native American Prayer

PRAYING FOR STUFF

Sometimes I forget
to consider the lilies
 of the field which neither
toil nor labor for their keep.

Part of me is always searching
for stuff instead of seeking
ways to improve the merchandise
of gratitude and prayer.

Some mornings, rather than fall
to my knees to give praise,
I scan the want ads for stuff.
Cheap stuff. Stuff for nothing.

Stuff enough to crowd out
the emptiness I know it brings.
Why can I never read a book
unless I know I own it?

It's the same with art, furniture,
and the sounds of electric pianos.
I have urges that want to walk
the corridors of divine mysteries

but spend my time gathering glitter.
Once I had a dream. I stepped before
the throne of God. He asked only
one question: "Did you become

who you were supposed to be?"
"I'm not sure," I told him.
"But when I died, I had so much stuff,
it took three days to find me."

—*Frederick Zydek*

FROM THE SINS THAT CLING SO CLOSELY

Lord, you know us so well, even our innermost
secrets, even parts of ourselves we do not know.

We are all too aware of the *warm* sins of old age: wasted time, the pursuit of trivialities, the cranky disposition, or the word spoken in anger. Make us aware of the *cold* sins of old age: our icy stares when someone offends us; our cool aloofness to strangers; our tendency to sit on our hands instead of standing for what is right; our preoccupation with our rights instead of what is right; our contentment with being lukewarm in devotion to you; our passivity when we are frozen by our fears. Forgive us, we pray, as we reach the end of life's day. Amen.

A SAINT'S PRAYER

O Lord, what will become of us?
We are so upset over a trivial loss.
We work so hard for a little money,
but take so little interest in caring for
   our souls.
We pay so little attention to unimpor-
   tant things
and practically forget what is really
   necessary.
We easily get lost in mundane
   concerns.
Help us recover our senses and return
   to you.

—*Thomas à Kempis, 1380–1471*

RENEWED DAY BY DAY

Father, help me to realize that even though I am growing older and my body is wearing out, this does not mean that I have to submit to the "myth of old age." It does not mean that my spirit is wearing out, too. Today will be soul day. I will watch the birds in their chattering flight to the feeder; I will write a soul friend; I will listen to great music that stirs my spirit; I will speak to someone at church whom I know is having a hard time; I will silently watch the sunset, and call my grandson. Amen.

INTERCESSION

Bountiful God, we pray for those who are stuck in their past, still brooding over old injuries, still dwelling on ancient wounds. *Bring to them a healing of memories.* We pray for those who face these later years with inadequate income and depleted resources or have abundant possessions but not enough peace. *Help them to know that their real treasure is in Heaven.* We pray for those who suffer chronic illnesses or who wait for test results, or who seem never to recover from their problems. *Grant them a sense of your presence.* We pray for those who find that life is more than they can handle, who get depressed and down-hearted. *Send them your spirit as Comforter.* In your strong name, we pray. Amen.

THE SHIP OF LIFE

Steer the ship of my life, good Lord,
to your quiet harbor,
where I can be safe from the storms of sin and
conflict.
Show me the course I should take.
Renew in me the gift of discernment,
so that I can always see the right direction in
which I should go.
And give me strength and the courage
to choose the right course,
even when the sea is rough and the waves are
high,
knowing that through enduring hardship and
danger
in your name
we shall find comfort and peace.

— Basil of Caesarea, c. 330–379

FOR DEEPER CONTEMPLATION

Gracious God, when we look at the life of Christ
or at some of the saints of the church we know
how far we fall short of your glory. We still
choose busy activity rather than contemplation;
we prefer our stuff rather than the simple life.
Even though life has slowed down we still want
to achieve and be in control, rather than lose our
lives for the gospel. Even now we want the good
life with all the comforts and conveniences,

rather than a life measured by character. Forgive us, Lord, and help us to seek the higher way. Amen.

WHEN INTERRUPTED

Merciful God, I am trying to deepen my inner life, to spend more time reading scripture and spiritual books, but I am so easily interrupted and distracted. The phone rings and someone wants me to listen. People stop by to share their stories, and my family demands so much time. I take courage in remembering that Jesus was often interrupted by human need. So much so, he had to withdraw to the mountains to be alone and pray. But there was no escape, even there. A father's cry for his epileptic son, the disciples' incessant questions, a woman at the well. Give me grace to see your presence in the spaces created by these interruptions. Amen.

DEAR LORD AND FATHER OF MANKIND

Dear Lord and Father of mankind,
forgive us our foolish ways,
reclothe us in our rightful mind,
in purer lives thy service find,
in deeper reverence praise.

In simple trust like theirs who heard,
beside the Syrian sea,

the gracious calling of the Lord,
let us, like them, without a word,
rise up and follow thee.

O sabbath rest by Galilee,
O calm of hills above,
where Jesus knelt to share with thee
the silence of eternity,
interpreted by love!

Drop thy still dews of quietness,
till all our strivings cease;
take from the souls the strain and stress,
and let our ordered lives confess,
the beauty of thy peace.

Breathe through the beats of our desire
thy coolness and thy balm;
let sense be dumb, let flesh retire;
speak through the earthquake, wind, and fire,
O still, small voice of calm. Amen.

—John Greenleaf Whittier, 1807–1892

LORD, THE SILENCE CALLS

Lord, every time I visit someone in the hospital I slip into the quiet chapel and pray. It's just for a few minutes that I stop there to talk with you. It is in the hush of that secluded place that I feel your nearness and the words of Jesus echo in my heart, "And whenever you pray, go into your

room and shut the door and pray to your Father who is in secret" (Matt. 6:6). *Everyone needs that upper room, that secret place, where we are truly alone with you.* As I grow older I know my need of prayer. Sometimes I feel it is because I know my mortality and there has to be something, *Someone,* beyond this time and space, more than my life here. I know I have more free time now, time at my command, and yet it is still so easy to get caught up in the frenetic busyness of retired life and forget these moments of quiet prayer. Lord, teach us to pray. Amen.

III.

ACCEPTING OUR AGING

Do not cast me off in the time of old age;
do not forsake me when my strength is spent.

—Psalm 71:9

MIRROR, MIRROR ON THE WALL

Lord, I looked at a picture of my old classmates at our forty-fifth reunion and said to my wife, "My, they look old!" She smiled and said, "Go look in the mirror!" And when I did I broke out laughing. Looking back at me was a seventy-year-old man with white hair—no ageless wonder. Looking into the mirror is a person who feels thirty, the same person I've always been. Forgive me, Lord, for trying to fool myself. I do look as old as my classmates, but I'm more myself now than I've ever been. Now we see in a mirror dimly, but then we will see face to face. We know that you look not at the outward appearance but rather at the heart. Amen.

LORD, HELP ME GET ON WITH MY LIFE

Lord, help me get off this aging elevator that carries me ever so swiftly from the basement of despair to the seventh floor of hope and then down to the basement again. My fists are tired of banging on the doors. Will I ever get off? I'm worn out from this up-and-down ride to nowhere. Help me to get off and get on with my life. Amen.

WHO'S AFRAID OF GETTING OLD? NOT ME!

Loving God, for years I was taught to dread getting old, as if long life was some incurable disease. For most people aging doesn't come easily. They would rather keep it at a distance, analyze it, delay it, anything but admit or touch it. They fear that getting old means blue hair or no hair at all, the loss of their mind, or endless pastimes to kill the time they have saved. But I am learning to accept my limitations, to cherish my white hair, and to actually to enjoy being older. So no face lifts, facial cremes, adjusted birth dates for me. I have been through enough battles to know what the warfare of life is about, and I will cherish my old age. Amen.

PRAYING HANDS

Christ, today I look at that incredible painting of an old man sitting before his meager meal with aged, gnarled praying hands. Hands tell much about a person. Your hands were marked by years of work in a carpenter's shop, making yokes for Galilean farms and furniture for Nazareth homes. How often those same hands blessed children and healed the sick. Your hands were nailed to a cross, and after the resurrection the disciples saw on them the nail prints. During your last appearance you lifted your hands in blessing as you left this world for eternity. Now we must be your hands of love and mercy to all whom we

meet. Help us, dear Jesus, to offer helping hands to others. Amen.

OLDER, NOT OLD

God of all ages, I am growing older. But help me never to be old. I am slower than I used to be, and I dread driving at night. I can remember scenes of long ago, but what I did yesterday easily slips from my mind. I find myself repeating the same old stories, and know it must bore people. You have spared me thus far from devastating illnesses, but I struggle every day with some trifling problem I used to take in stride. May my spirit never age, but grow younger as the days wind down. I may not run fast any longer, but help me walk into the sunset years. In you, who promised that "they will mount up with wings like eagles, . . . they shall walk and not faint" (Isa. 40:31), I pray. Amen.

WE BRING TO OLD AGE

Father of mercies, now that I am older I begin to realize who I am now is the person I have always been. I know there are some new tricks you can teach this old man, but in many ways I am spiritually now what I was in earlier days. Now that the autumn of life is here and winter seems so close, I am grateful for the times I took to be with you during the spring and summer years. It is

never too late to turn to you; but when we are older we really see you as an old friend who has been with us from childhood. So I pause now to give thanks for your unfailing companionship on this journey we call life. You have sustained me—never forsaken or failed me—and been my best friend. I can say with the psalmist, *"You guide me with your counsel, and afterwards you will take me into glory. Whom have I in heaven but you, and being with you, I desire nothing on earth"* (Ps. 73:24-25, NIV). Amen.

GROWING OLDER

When the signs of age begin to mark my body (and still more when they touch my mind); when the ill that is to diminish me or carry me off strikes from without or is born within me; when the painful moment comes in which I suddenly awaken to the fact that I am ill or growing old; and above all at that last moment when I feel I am losing hold of myself and am absolutely passive within the hands of the great unknown forces that have formed me; in all those dark moments, O God, grant that I may understand that it is you (provided only my faith is strong enough) who are painfully parting the fibres of my being in order to penetrate to the very marrow of my substance and bear me away within yourself.

— *Pierre Teilhard de Chardin, 1881–1955*

ACCEPTING MY LIMITATIONS

Loving God, today I acknowledge my limitations. I admit that sometimes I think I am still a young man—dashing off to do work, expending energy to accomplish my projects, and then wondering why I am so tired. Perhaps it is because I am painfully aware of my mortality. Friends my age are dying every day, and my relentless busyness seems a way to ward off my finitude. Help me, I pray, to accept my limitations. Help me to find that peaceful release that comes with those limitations. May I find peace in knowing I don't have to be everyone's problem-solver or project director. Give me the peace that came to the psalmist when he wrote, "I do not concern myself with great matters, or things too wonderful for me. But I have stilled and quieted my soul" (Ps. 131:2, NIV). This I pray as I now walk and can no longer run. Amen.

WHEN ANXIOUS

Lord, now that I am older it is difficult to have a moment's peace. It seems I worry about everything, and when everything seems all right I worry that there is nothing to worry about. Lord, I give you now my anxiety and my torments: the fear that every time the phone rings some catastrophe has happened; the fear that every ache I get is a symptom of some dreaded disease; the anxiety that I may have to go to a nursing home

someday; the troubles of the day that I go over and over in bed at night. Lord, help me to give my cares to you. I need your help. Amen.

TOO LATE, AND YET . . .

Dear God, I've been reading Alan Paton's book, *Too Late the Phalarope*, and it has spoken to me at this time in my life. I am in the twilight of my life, and I fully know my limitations. I cannot be like some older people, who pretend they are twenty-three and try to give the impression that they will never be older. I know I am older. I know I have slowed down and cannot do what I used to do. No fooling myself or anyone else that I am not growing older. I accept this. My only twinge of sadness is that it is too late . . . too late to fulfill some of my dreams and hopes. I sometimes wince when I realize that *if* I were only younger, possessed with the wisdom and maturity I now have, what a success I might be. But now I am too old and it is too late. Help me not to drown in self-pity or remorse over what might have been. Help me to be thankful for my life thus lived and to seize this moment to be what I can by your grace. In the name of the One who alone understands. Amen.

FOR PROTECTION

Protector God, we are often worried about our safety. Growing older means we know full well what the psalmist wrote, "But for me, my feet had almost stumbled; my steps had nearly slipped" (Ps. 78:2). We fear every day the fall that will force us into dependency and hasten our frailty. We hear horror stories about threats to the security of older people. We remember those sunny days when we left the doors of our homes unlocked, but now we need dead bolt locks to keep out intruders. May we find security where we live and realize that our utmost security is in you, the God who preserves us from evil and stands watch over our lives. Amen.

WHEN I HAVE TO USE A WALKER

Lord, I am struggling with this infirmity of old age and get so frustrated that I have to use a walker. Doesn't anyone know that I used to walk three miles a day, and now it is a struggle to walk around my house? So many people see me in terms of what I cannot do, rather than as the person I am. It seems that their blindness is in their fear that this will happen to them—their wings will be clipped and their steps slowed to a crawl. Forgive them, Lord, but forgive me too. I know I have reacted to frail people this way too. But no more. Amen.

LORD, I FELL TODAY

Caring God, I fell. Such a careless, dumb mistake. I was in a hurry, not watching where I was going, and severely injured my ankle. Now, weeks later, I am more and more impatient as the healing takes so long. I want a quick fix, a magic shot that will restore me to my earlier pace. I've prayed for a cure, but it doesn't happen. I feel I am stuck with this thorn in my flesh. Growing older means we don't recover from falls as quickly—it takes time. So, like your servant Jacob, I limp along, realizing that slowing down is not a sin and our wounds can become places of new beginnings. Amen.

GIVE ME PATIENCE . . . NOW!

Lord, I know you care about me. You clothe the lilies with dazzling white and feed the birds through human hands. But I become impatient when life moves so slowly. At times I feel like the children of Israel, who wandered in the wilderness for forty years. I want to ask you the question of a little child on a long trip, "Are we there yet?" I want detailed maps of my journey, and assurance that I will get there without delay. But there are no shortcuts. The detours I detest will lead to places of grace. Be patient with me, Lord, even when my patience wears thin. Amen.

GOD, MAKE ME LAUGH

God, make me laugh at myself. Make me laugh when I can't seem to remember names and am embarrassed. Make me laugh when I stumble and fall and barely catch myself. Make me laugh when someone calls me "an old person" and it makes me mad. Make me laugh when I say something stupid or spill food on the floor. You who made the mountains and made us from dust, you can! Amen.

DEPENDING ON OTHERS

Loving Parent, when I was a child I was afraid to be alone. I remember one day when I got lost in a big department store and cried my heart out until my parents found me. Later in life I learned to be independent, to enjoy solitude, and to relish moments spent alone without the clamor of other voices or the clatter of things. When I became older I thought I could be independent, but I've learned also to depend on others for help.

But old age triggers those buried childhood fears of being alone. When my wife and I are separated for a few days I get a panic attack and regress back to my childhood fear of abandonment. Life is hard. Just when we thought we had it all together, old baggage returns to plague us and we carry it into anxious days and sleepless nights. Help me, Father, to realize it is okay to

depend on others, to shed my stupid armor of self-importance that makes me think I am invincible. Help me also to honor those moments when I am alone, knowing nothing can separate me from your love. Amen.

A LITTLE PRAYER

Lord, you have shared our life in all its stages
    and you experienced old age.
Do not let me become a grumpy old man,
always complaining, quarreling, and criticizing,
a burden to himself and others.
Let me go on laughing and smiling. . . .
Let me keep my sense of humor,
so that I can put people—and myself—
    in the right place,
laugh at my own faults, and joke about
    my sufferings.
Make me, Lord, a smiling old man,
who, though he can no longer give much
    to his brothers,
can at least give them a little joy.

. . . .

Lord, you are eternally present.
Do not let me become an old man who lives in
    the past,
always talking about the good old times when
    it was never cold
and disliking the present time of young people,
    when it is always raining.

Make me live my past again with happiness,
but let me also love and understand the
      present,
which is yours like the past and the future.
Let me be the old man, Lord, who has not
      forgotten his youth,
and who makes others feel young.

Lord, you have established the seasons of the
      year and the seasons of man's life.
Let me be a man of all seasons.
I don't ask you for happiness,
because I know only too well that no season
      will bring it,
not even spring.
But I do ask that the last season of my life
      may be fine;
so it will bear witness to your beauty.

—*Joseph Folliet (Brother Juniper)*

DEPRESSED

I'm back again in a depressed mood. For a while
I thought I had licked the problem, but now it
covers me like a black cloud. This mood
dampens my spirit and makes me sad. Maybe
it's the awareness of how much of life has gone
and how little remains. Maybe it's because my
children and grandchildren are so far away, and
I don't see them that often. Maybe it's because
some people think that I am on the sidelines,

and I am only called upon in emergencies. Yet I remember a time, dear Lord, when you felt despair in a garden called Gethsemane. You prayed that the cup would pass. Your closest friends slept while you agonized alone. What keeps me on center is realizing that since you knew that awful loneliness, we never have to be alone. Amen.

PRAYERS IN THE NIGHT

O Lord, you are my keeper by day and at night. I've come to that time in my old age when sleep often forsakes me and leaves me wide awake in those darkest and most interminable hours of the night—from two to five. At times I confess I toss and tumble, like a fish out of water. But I am learning to use those sleepless hours to retrace my childhood and revisit wonderful landscapes that I remember from life's journey. And I am learning something new about prayer in those eyes-wide-open night hours: I am learning that I am not so much praying as being prayed through, and that there is a haunting presence that keeps guard duty over my life. Such prayer is like the Spirit; it is not at our command. It comes and goes. But when it happens, it is enough. I have caught a glimpse of what prayer is. Amen.

PRAYER OF AN AGING WOMAN

Lord, you know better than I know myself that I am growing older and will someday be old. Keep me from being talkative and particularly from the fatal habit of thinking that I must say something on every subject and on every occasion.

Release me from craving to straighten out everybody's affairs. Make me thoughtful but not moody; helpful but not bossy. With my vast store of wisdom, it seems a pity not to use it all, but you know, Lord, that I want a few friends at the end. Keep my mind from the recital of endless details—give me wings to come to the point.

I ask for grace enough to listen to the tales of others' pain. But seal my lips on my own aches and pains—they are increasing, and my love of rehearsing them is becoming sweeter as the years go by. Help me to endure them with patience.

I dare not ask for improved memory but for a growing humility and a lessening cocksureness when my memory seems to clash with the memories of others. Teach me the glorious lesson that occasionally it is possible that I might be mistaken.

Keep me reasonably sweet. I do not want to be a saint—some of them are so hard to live with—but a sour old woman is one of the crowning works of the devil!

Give me the ability to see good things in unexpected places, and talents in unexpected people. And give me, O Lord, the grace to tell them so.

—Attributed to a seventeenth-century nun

PRAYER OF AN AGING MAN

Living Christ, how difficult it is to be an aging man. For so many years I was the one in charge, and now I stand behind the scenes while others are in control. Give me the humility to play second fiddle, and not worry about who gets the credit if you get the glory. I ask for grace to be willing to step aside and let younger people be in control. Although I am not ready to quit, I need to withdraw and let others do the job. Give me patience with those who would use or refuse me, and let me see their rejection as a reflection on them, not me. Let me savor the slowed-down pace of life, cultivate my inner life, and be glad that I am not always on call anymore. Amen.

PRAYER FOR LIFE'S LATER YEARS

Each stage of life is a gift with different graces and challenges and today we thank you for the gift of the latter years of life. We are grateful for days of retirement when we are given time to enjoy the grandchildren, pick up the project we started ten years ago, travel and enjoy the various cultures and peoples of the world, learn a new skill, serve at the soup kitchen, wield a hammer for Habitat, engage in intercessory prayer.

We thank you for this time when we may pause from the busyness of life long enough to learn that our hearts still beat with compassion, our

hands still yearn to reach out in service, and our minds are as hungry as ever for your Word. . . .

Because we trust our relationship with you, we open our hearts honestly and offer to you our frustrations and discouragements as well. We are offended by those who would talk to us as though we are infantile. Our hearing may be failing, our vision fading, but O God, we have our dignity, we have lessons to share, we have gifts to give. We are angry and weary when our days are cut short by Alzheimer's, strokes, and other degenerative illnesses. We grieve the losses that come so quickly now—the driver's license, the ability to get out of the chair easily and quickly, the capacity to care for our homes, the loss of our homes, the death that takes our spouse, our friends.

We cry out and wait for strength to be renewed; for weariness and mourning to be replaced by comfort and joy and faintness to be lost in hope.

We do place our lives in your hands, O God, because we know that with you the final word is life. Amen.

—*Beth Ann Miller*

ON READING PSALM 139

O Lord, you have searched me and you know me. You know when I sit and when I rise (and when I am older, it is easier to sit than stand).

You perceive my thoughts from afar (even when they are muddled and I can't remember what happened yesterday). You discern my going out and my lying down (especially when I stumble, lose my balance, or use a walker or sit in my geri-chair). You are familiar with all my ways (yes, even when I forget things and deny my aging). Before a word is on my tongue you know it completely, O Lord (even when I tell people exactly what I think!). You hem me in behind and before; you have laid your hand upon me. (Lord, how many times have you prevented me from falling or making a fool of myself?) Such knowledge is too wonderful for me, too lofty for me to attain. Where can I go from your Spirit? Where can I flee from your presence? If I go up to the heavens you are there; if I make my bed in the depths you are there (even if I make my bed in a nursing home). If I rise on the wings of dawn, if I settle on the far side of the sea, (and it will seem like that if/when I leave my home), even there you will guide me; your right hand will hold me fast. If I say "Surely the darkness (the depression and feelings of worthlessness that darken my days) will hide me," even the darkness will not be dark to you (there is nothing I experience, however dark, that is unknown to you). How precious to me are your thoughts, O God! How vast is the sum of them! (Other people ignore me, waste me, use me, but you love and cherish me.) Search me, O God, and know my heart; test me and know my anxious thoughts.

See if there is any offensive way in me, and lead me in the way everlasting.

MY SYMPHONY

Dear God,
Help me
To live content with small means,
to seek elegance rather than luxury,
and refinement rather than fashion,
to be worthy, not respectable, and
    wealthy, not rich,
to study hard, think quietly,
    talk gently, act frankly,
to listen to stars and birds, babes and
    sages, with open
     heart,
to bear all cheerfully,
do all bravely,
await occasions,
hurry never—
in a word, to let the spiritual, unbidden
and
    unconscious,
grow up through the common.
This is to be my symphony.
Amen.

—*William Ellery Channing, 1780–1842*

PRAYER OF THE THIRD AGE

Lord, teach me how to grow old!

Convince me that the community does me no wrong if it lifts responsibilities from my back, no longer asks my advice, and finds others to take my place.

Take from me the pride of experience and the sense of my indispensability. May I be able to accept, in this gradual detachment from things, what is simply the law of time; and may I be able to see in this change in my duties one of the most fascinating manifestations of life renewed by your Providence.

Keep me, O Lord, useful to the world, contributing by my optimism and my prayers to the joy and the courage of those who are now in the harness of responsibility; and make me humble and serene in my contact with the changing world, having no regrets for the past, offering my sufferings as a gift for the reconciliation of society. May my leaving the field of action be simple and natural, like the gentle setting of the sun.

Forgive me if only today, in tranquillity, I understand how much you have loved me and helped me. At least in this moment may I have a clear and full perception of the destiny of incredible joy you have prepared for me, and towards which you have set me walking since the very first day of my life.

Lord, teach me how to grow old like this! Amen.

—*Anonymous*

LORD OF THE SEASONS

Summer has ended and the leaves begin their inevitable descent to the earth. There is a touch of autumn in the air, reminding us that winter is not far away. A gentle hush seems to fill our days and nights, as if life has slowed down and the harvest has come. I confess that I cling to each day—like the last leaf that clings to the oak tree, refusing to fall to the ground. I want every day to stretch out forever, knowing full well what winter means. Open my heart to the beauties of golden autumn, and give me hope that beyond the coming winter there is an invincible spring that lasts forever. Amen.

IV.

DISCERNING THE MEANING OF OUR STORIES

*I consider the days of old, and remember
the years of long ago: I commune with my heart
in the night; I meditate and search my spirit.*

—Psalm 77:5-6

REMEMBERING

Gracious God, somewhere I've read that as I grow older I should preserve my memories, for they are all that is left. Lord, I do cherish my memories, for they tell me who I have been and assure me of who I am now. But there is more to life than memories. I live now, not then. Every day until I leave this earth is a new opportunity to create memories. And all around me are people in need. As I reach out to help I am creating new memories for the years that lie ahead. Amen.

NOSTALGIA

Dear God, I wandered into the church sanctuary as they decorated the Christmas tree with chrismons. It's that time again. I wanted to linger and watch but it was too painful. Chrismons always conjure up old memories that are sharp as a two-edged sword. Lonely seasons, rejected gifts, empty places at the table. These memories descend on me like a sudden wave, almost engulfing me, and I want to forget. . . . And then I remember Bethlehem. Amen.

GOD AT WORK IN MY LIFE

I can see clearly now what I saw only dimly in the past: that you, O God, have been at work in my life. I used to think that my life was a series of random acts of will or good luck, but not now. I look at my faith journey and I can see how you have been at work from my birth to the present time.

The ancient psalmist was right: "My times are in your hand" (Ps. 31:15). Everything I thought was deviation or a wrong turn was part of your plan. I now see how you lovingly used every thread of my life to weave the fabric that is my story. So I surrender to you, knowing that—even now—as long as I choose to grow, you, God, will show the way; and that as a tree must grow towards the light, so must I grow toward you. Amen.

ON LOOKING AT OLD SCRAPBOOKS

Lord of history, I took my old scrapbooks out of the trunk and was amazed at what they told me. Faded, yellowed pictures of days gone by; photographs of parents wearing bygone clothes; pictures of me in childhood dress, at places now clouded by the past. Yet this is my history, my story. But I am "more than who I was"; I am me. Amen.

THE TREE HAS NEVER BLOOMED

With tears running, O Great Spirit,
Great Spirit, my Grandfather,
—with running tears I must say now
that the tree has never bloomed.
You see me here, an old man. Here at the
    center
of the world, where you took me
when I was young and taught me;
here old, I stand,
and the tree is withered,
Grandfather, my Grandfather!

Again,
and maybe the last time on this earth,
I recall the great vision you sent me.
It may be
that some little root of the sacred tree still lives.
Nourish it then,
that it may leaf and bloom and fill with
    singing birds,
Hear me, not for myself, but for my people;
I am old. Hear me
that they may once more go back into the
    sacred hoop
and find the good red road,
the shielding tree!

   —*Black Elk: Oglala Sioux tradition, 1863–1950*

MY LIFE STORY

Gracious God, I have tried since my "retirement" to write my life story, but it seems that life interrupts me again and again. It seems I write new chapters to this book all the time, and the time grows short for me to get this task completed. I know that this is the legacy I leave, my story. Deliver me from the busyness that takes me away from this task and the presumption that I have all the time in the world left to do it. Let me see the writing of my story as a thank-you note for your grace and help along the journey of life and as a gift to my family. Pardon the delay, Lord. I will begin again to write my story. Amen.

LORD OF HISTORY

At times I feel like Ebenezer Scrooge, as memories of my past return at night in recognizable dreams, and during the daylight hours as sounds or smells of former years send me spinning into yesterday. We are not stuck in our past, but recalling our stories reveals who we are now. *For all that we remember with joy,* we thank you God, for all kind persons who made those memories possible. *For all that we remember with sadness,* we thank you God, for pain that taught us patience. *For all we remember with resentment,* forgive them, O Lord, and help us not to be grudge-keepers. *For all we remember that we would rather forget*—old resentments, lingering crises—

help us to see these in the light of your providence, as crucial pieces of our life puzzle. So, may remembering our stories bring us courage to live out our present stories. May we realize that your story of love redeems the whole story. Amen.

FAMILY REUNION

We gathered for a family reunion from across the country. We paraded old photos of yesteryear and played old tapes of former celebrations. But it was not the same. The years have taken their toll and our memories are fragile. Stories were told in different ways, each according to his or her own perception. As an ancient writer once said, "We do not see things as they are, but as we are." But we laughed and toasted our parents, even though the years have blurred our memories and distorted our views. Some day we shall see and understand, even as we are fully understood. Amen.

THERE ARE NO ACCIDENTS

It came like a flash of light, a real "Aha!" experience. I had viewed my life only as a disconnected series of events, a jumbled puzzle of ups and downs. I had been so busy living my life, I had no time to look at what it meant. Then, as I recalled crucial times—dead-ends and

new beginnings—I realized that there are no accidents. What I thought was coincidence became a grace moment, and I could say with Jacob of old, "Surely the Lord is in this place— and I did not know it!" (Gen. 28:16). Thank you for showing me that it all makes sense. Amen.

A LIFELINE

Lord, I look back at my life and remember former years long past. What lies ahead? The end of the line is death. Only you know that date, but it makes me realize how important the time is between now and then. I don't want to drift in these last years, but to make the most of all opportunities. I must make plans and not be a victim of indecision or waste. So, Lord, here in your presence I make a time line, and plan for what is left of my life. Amen.

FOR A DAY OF REMEMBRANCE

You have given me memories to hold, and I cherish that which I have known and loved. You have taught me how to keep alive the lingering poetry of time and place. You have enabled me to recall the green of spring when winter comes, and the lushness of summer when December is barren and cold. You have given me the memory of faces and voices, the remembrance of hands once touched, and of laughter and tears once

shared. I am thankful for all good memories of this day—for people I have known, for streets I have walked, and for houses I have lived in. You have given me so much, O Lord, and I spend so little time in remembering. Let me remember yesterday, and let me anticipate tomorrow, through Jesus Christ our Lord. Amen.

I REMEMBER OLD HOMES

Gracious God, tonight I remember the homes where I have lived. That manse with the white picket fence—life was simpler in my old Kentucky home. I remember the rock stone house where I spent my boyhood days . . . never apart from the church. I recall the lonely one-room apartment where I forged a new life; small as it was, it was my staying place for awhile. I think now of this home, where I am spending the later years of my life. There is a quiet solemnity here. The children's voices are gone. And yet here in these twilight years there is a beauty, a light no darkness can destroy. Still, dear Lord, I am never really at home here. There is a God-shaped space in my heart, and I know I am but a stranger in this world. My real home is with you. Amen.

THANKS FOR THE MEMORIES

Friend of the aged, today I ran into an old friend whom I hadn't seen for twenty years. We'd lost touch, but seeing her rekindled memories of good times. We really don't keep our friendships up to date. So it is good to remember those souls who have touched my life. They listened when everyone else wanted to give advice. They let me tell my story, and never told me theirs. They cared, when others passed by on the other side. Their non-anxious presence was "balm in Gilead," and brought me beyond my worries and fears. Thank you, Lord, for coming in the flesh in Jesus, and thank you for coming again in those Christlike souls who came to my side. Amen.

STORY TIME AGAIN

Father of Mercies, it fascinates me that as we grow older we love to tell our grandchildren stories about when we were growing up. I can hear their laughter as I told them about the parrot who spoke with a British accent, and how once my father broke a window at the church playing baseball. My grandchildren loved those stories because they made me human. But why don't we tell them "growing down" stories? Would they love to hear what it means to grow older, to be more dependent on others, to live as an older person today? Let me tell those stories, too . . . and help them to understand me better. Amen.

WISDOM KEEPERS

Their hair is snow-white, their eyes have grown cloudy, and they don't go out much anymore. It's so easy to breeze right past them and never look into those old eyes. But, Lord, when they stop me and I really listen, what wonderful stories they tell. Old schoolhouses and 1916 floods, surreys with fringe on top, and kerosene lamps. Protracted revivals and funeral fans. When I listen, their eyes light up, and at times I think they will jump out of their skins. Lord, forgive me for not listening. Thank you for these tellers of stories and preservers of history. Amen.

BLESSING A GRANDCHILD

May the spirit of God be your guide all through your days. May you know long life and abundant grace and God's presence to sustain you in times of trouble and surround you in all of life's ventures. May you walk in the paths of righteousness doing justice, loving kindness, and walking humbly with your God. May the God in whose hands are our times keep you forever. Amen.

BROKEN FRIENDSHIPS

Dear God,
Lover of us all,
do not let me go down into the grave
with old broken friendships unresolved.
Give to us and to all with whom
we have shared our lives
and deepest selves
along the Way,
the courage not only to express anger
when we feel let down,
but your more generous love
which always seeks to reconcile
and so to build a more enduring love
between those we have held dear
as friends.

—*Kathy Keay*

DELIVER ME, O LORD GOD

Loving Christ, Love Divine, all loves excelling, you alone know my inmost thoughts, the deep places of my soul, and you know how hard it is for me to forgive _____ for what this person did to me. I have tried to justify my resentment by saying *I am in the right*, but down deep I know this is not right, and admit I am a grudge-keeper. I hold on to my resentment like a dog clutches a bone. The acid of my bitterness has eroded my spirit, and I want to be free of it. Help

me to forgive _____. Part of me wants to keep this grudge, but another part wants to let it go. Make my divided will submit to your will. Make me quick to see my own faults, "the log in my eye," and look beyond the splinter in others' eyes. Help me realize that only as I forgive _____ will I be forgiven. Give me grace to pray this prayer. Lord, treat me tomorrow as I treat my enemies today. Amen.

AWESOME GOD

It is so easy to look at my problems and complain. And it is even easier to sit around and do nothing of value. I know that three great temptations of older people are to whine, shine, or recline. Deliver me from being a whiner or a couch potato. And I don't even want to shine, but to simply be there as a person who lives to enjoy life and help others. When I look at the simple goodness of so many people, the beauty of your world and the joy found in grandchildren and simple things, I can only exclaim, *God, the wonders there are! God, the wonders there are!* Amen.

PRECIOUS MEMORIES

Ancient of Days, you have entrusted me with precious memories. As I grow older my short-term memory fails. I can't remember where I

parked my car or what I did yesterday. But memories of the past are as clear as a bell. I recall my childhood, when life was not so frantic and frenetic. I can revisit the family fun around the table, the jokes, the neighbors' visits. I can hear my father reading the psalms and my mother's prayers. Why has life changed so much? Have we gained the whole world and lost our souls? We have so many electronic devices and so little life of the soul. We can e-mail our messages with the rapidity of lightning, and yet still are strangers to one another. Jet planes fly us with amazing speed, and still we are not sure where we are going. Thank you, God, for our past; I don't want to stay there, but it helps to remember. It makes me aware of who I was, and am. Amen.

WHATEVER IS—IS BEST

I know, as my life grows older,
　　And mine eyes have clearer sight,
That under each rank wrong some
　　　　where
　　There lies the root of Right;

That each sparrow has its purpose,
　　By the sorrowing oft unguessed;
But as sure as the sun brings morning,
　　Whatever is—is best.

I know that each sinful action,

As sure as the night brings shade,
Is somewhere, sometime punished
    Tho' the hour be long delayed.
I know that the soul is aided
    Sometimes by the heart's unrest,
And to grow means often to suffer—
    But whatever is—is best.

I know there are no errors,
    In the great Eternal plan,
And all things work together
    For the final good of man.

And I know when my soul speeds
        onward,
    In its grand Eternal quest,
I shall say as I look back earthward,
    Whatever is—is best.

—*Ella Wheeler Wilcox*

V.

MENTORING THE NEXT GENERATIONS

So even to old age and gray hairs,
O God, do not forsake me, until I proclaim
your might to all the generations to come.

—Psalm 71:18

PRAYER FOR FACES YET NOT SEEN

Think not forever of yourselves, O Chiefs,
nor of your own generation.
Think of continuing generations of our families,
think of our grandchildren
and of those yet unborn,
whose faces are coming from
beneath the ground.

—The Peacemaker
Founder of the Iroquois Confederacy, c. 1000

PRAYER FOR THE COMING GENERATIONS

Grandfather God, these ancient words make me aware of my need to prepare the way for coming generations. As I grow older I become less preoccupied with myself and more concerned about the generations yet to come. Teach me wisdom to give to my grandchildren and those yet unborn, that they may see in me a worthy example of truth and goodness. Help me to show compassion and love in word and deed, to tell these children about your presence through good and bad times. In so doing I will leave that legacy of which your ancient sage wrote, "A good name is to be chosen rather than great riches" (Prov. 22:1). Amen.

RECEIVING AND LEAVING

Lord of history, when our ancestors die our identities are broken, our roots laid bare with little protection from the storms of life. We feel like motherless children. Yet we know that it is their leaving that makes us discover the sacredness of our own stories and our need to leave our wisdom and experience to our own children. Help us to share our stories with those who will come after us, and to point them back to their spiritual heritage. In this way may we bless them as they make their own journey through this land. Amen.

ACROSS GENERATIONS

Lord of generations, help those who are young to help those of us who are older. We want to feel needed and to have a valuable role in society. Help us to realize our responsibilities to society, that we will not just rest on our laurels from past times. May those who are young realize the wisdom of older people, because we have lived. May those of us who are older be mentors by our example. Grant, O Lord, that we may see all people—young or old—as the persons they are; not as an old person or young person, but simply as a child of God to be treated with dignity and respect. Amen.

GOD OF THE GENERATIONS

Loving God, how beautiful are the young—so full of life and joy, whose strong bodies sway in the dance of life. From them we learn to live life to the fullest, seize the moment, and care little for the trifling things. Loving God, how beautiful are we who are old. Our skills have helped us survive the harsh shocks of adversity and our wisdom takes the bitter and sweet, to weave a rich tapestry of patterns all its own. May we truly learn from each other and walk hand in hand through this land. Amen.

BECOMING A MENTOR TO THE COMING GENERATIONS

There are times, Understanding God, when I feel of no use to anyone now that I am old. I excuse my laziness by thinking I have been passed by for younger people. Help me to realize that I have much to offer. Give me the eyes of the heart to find children to whom I can offer my wisdom and experiences and guide them into your way. Make me an instrument of your grace. Help me in a quiet, loving way to share the lessons of life I have learned, and in so doing to make rough places smooth for all children. Amen.

ON LEAVING FOOTPRINTS
FOR THOSE WHO FOLLOW

Loving Parent, you have entrusted to me the precious souls of my grandchildren and their children yet to be born. I want them to grow up to be fair and fine and free. Yet they have so many temptations and distractions that never afflicted me. So I pray for myself, that I may set before these children an example to follow. May they see in my life the fruit of the Spirit: love, joy, peace, long-suffering, kindness, goodness, faithfulness, gentleness, and self-control. That will be the best legacy I can leave them. Amen.

LONG-DISTANCE PRAYERS

Loving God, how difficult it is to be so far away from my grandchildren. They have moved across the country, and I only see them twice a year. They grow so quickly, and how I miss being a vital part of their lives right now. So I call them, send them gifts and letters, plead with their parents for up-to-date pictures, and hope they remember me. I stay in touch by prayer— praying for them by name every day and night and asking God to help them grow and become strong in spirit, filled with wisdom and the grace of God. Help me to realize that although we may be absent from each other, separated by thousands of miles, I can still make them aware of my love for them. Amen.

PASSING ON THE STORY

Gracious God, help me to see myself as the family storyteller. Every family has a story, and each child needs someone to tell the story and to draw that child into the story. Help me to share our stories of happy times as well as experiences of pain and loss. Help me to be honest and not hide the truth that later might hurt their own growth. As they hear these stories, I launch them toward their own stories. Amen.

A PRAYER FOR THE FUTURE

You must teach your children that the ground between their feet is the ashes of our ancestors. So that they will respect the land, tell your children that the earth is rich with the lives of our kin. Teach your children what we have taught our children, that the earth is our mother. Whatever befalls the earth befalls the children of the earth.

This we know. The earth does not belong to us; we belong to the earth. This we know. All things are connected like the blood which unites one family. All things are connected. Whatever befalls the earth befalls the children of the earth. We do not weave the web of life, we are merely a strand in it. Whatever we do to the web, we do to ourselves.

—*Attributed to Chief Seattle, c. 1786–1866*

MENTORS NEEDED

God of all wisdom, I look around and see so many children who need guidance. They are like a young tree with its roots laid bare and no support against the howling wind. They need a friend who will guide them, who will share time with them and tell them stories. They need a person wise from years of experience and patient from times of trouble. They need a person who knows you, Lord, and can make you real. They want someone who will care about them, love them unconditionally, and make them aware of the meaning of life. Am I that someone, Lord? Amen.

THANKS FOR BRIDGES

We give thanks, O Creator God, for people in our experience who have been bridges, helping us from here to there, at times over troubled waters. Thank you for our mentors and helpers, who opened the way from a dead past to a better future. How can we express our gratitude, Lord? By being bridges for others of coming generations. Help us to escape from the narrow prison of self. May we become bridges over which the coming generations will walk to a brighter tomorrow. Amen.

FOR YOUNG PERSONS

God our Father, you see your children growing up in an unsteady and confusing world: Show them that your ways give more life than the ways of the world, and that following you is better than chasing after selfish goals. Help them to take failure, not as a measure of their worth, but as a chance for a new start. Give them strength to hold their faith in you, and to keep alive their joy in your creation; through Jesus Christ our Lord. Amen.

—Episcopal Church of the United States of America, Book of Common Prayer

PRAYER FOR LITTLE CHILDREN

Merciful Parent, if not even a sparrow falls to the ground without your care, how much more you love all the little children of the world. Watch over them in their innocence. Protect them as they skip down the street. Protect them as they scamper in their homes. Protect them from all abuse. Keep them from any who would do them evil, and surround them with your pillar of fire and cloud by night. This I ask in the name of Jesus, who chided the disciples for rebuking the children and always welcomed them into his arms. Amen.

FATHER, FORGIVE

Forgiving God, you have searched me and there is not a thought in my mind or an experience from my past unknown to you. As I reflect on my life I confess that my pursuit of success and preoccupation with my work deprived my children of my presence when they were young. But now, Lord, later in life I have tried to make amends by caring about my children's children. Freed from anxiety about their behavior or concern for my own reputation, I can be myself with them. Help me, dear Lord, to pass on to them the enduring values that have nourished my life. May they realize from my example that life does not consist in fleeting success or momentary things, but in "doing justice, loving kindness, and walking humbly with you, God" (Mic. 6:8, paraphrase). Amen.

FOR THE NEXT GENERATIONS

Lord God, the generations are in your hands, and your hands are love. We thank you for the wisdom and truth each new generation inherits from the past. Yet our responsibility to hand down this legacy frightens us. Our children's use of their inheritance depends so much on the way we pass it on. Show us, Father, how to do this confidently and not anxiously. Help us to avoid allowing our words to tell one story while our actions tell another. Help us not to hand down

ready-made answers or pious platitudes, but rather to pass on the wisdom we have learned through experience. Amen.

A TEENAGER'S PRAYER

Dear God,
There have been many times in history when you have been portrayed as an old man: the white hair, wrinkled face, and feeble-looking body covered with a flowing robe. Yet, you are all-powerful and all-knowing. Sometimes, on earth, we take our elderly people for granted. We think of them as a waste of time and a waste of money. But maybe if we took a few moments to talk to and listen to older people, we could save a lot of time and money. Give us patience, God, to listen and to learn. Give us tolerance when we don't understand. And give us love so that we may care for older people and so that the next generation will already know what it is taking us so long to learn. Amen.

—Kim Richardson
Cardinal Gibbons High School, Raleigh, NC

LORD, HELP ME TO GIVE THE RIGHT ANSWER

My ten-year-old grandson, Daniel, asked me a great question, Lord: "Grandpa, you seem to have a happy, good life. Will my life be as good as yours?" For a moment I paused. He kept on asking penetrating questions. "What lies ahead? What will it be like in the twenty-first century when I am older? Will the world be safer than now? Will cancer and heart disease be at an end? Do you think I might go into outer space?" I told him, Lord, that, yes, he would have a good life, and I hoped he would be happy and well. I told him that if he was a good man, loved his family, and trusted in God he would be happy. He smiled. I didn't answer those questions, but it still was a powerful moment between generations. We valued each other, and somehow the gap between us seemed a lot smaller. Thank you, Lord. Amen.

A REAL HERITAGE

Today, Lord, I've been reading from the Book of Ecclesiasticus. I know that book never got into our Bible, but sometimes I wonder why. I read the words

> *"Now will I praise . . . our ancestors.*
> *Their wealth remains in their families,*
> *their heritage with their descendants;*
> *Through God's covenant with them*
> *their family endures,*
>
> . . . .
> *Their bodies are peacefully laid away,*
> *but their name lives on and on."*

(Sirach 44:1, 11-12, 14, NAB)

I gave thanks for my ancestors and for the way they have influenced my life. I pray with all of my heart that I may entrust the same values and faith to my children and grandchildren, so that in years to come they will remember me with thanksgiving. Amen.

A TOUCH OF GRACE

Blessed Grandfather, I love little children and I miss my grandchildren who live so far away. Today my arthritis was killing me, and I felt tired and old. I had to go to a Christmas party, and put on my clown face as we sang "Joy to the World." Suddenly a little girl walked from the children's choir, hugged me, and whispered, "Merry Christmas, Grandpa!" Such a serendipitous moment. I didn't even know her name, but for a moment I felt I *was* her Grandpa. I know we are supposed to be examples for coming generations, but this time I received the gift. Thank you, God, for the honesty, love, and transparency of little children. Coming from across the crowded room a little stranger hugged me, and I felt renewed in spirit. Amen.

THE PLEAS OF A LOST CHILD

Dear Parent to us all, welcome home all of us prodigals who have taken our inheritance and wasted it recklessly. For we are weary and have

need of your outstretched arms—reaching for us before lecturing, enfolding us with your grace when we deserved punishment, celebrating our awakening when it would have been more just to remind us of our shortcomings. O Mother/Father of our wayward years, teach us that though we have left the haven of your compassion, you have never been far away, for your law has been planted in our hearts and your strength left in our minds that we might seek its source. And even at the lowest points of our lives apart from you, we have never been abandoned, but have sensed the still, small voice that is yours. You gave us freedom that we might find forgiveness. You gave us minds that we might learn our limits. You gave us despair that we might learn of hope. You gave us the wilderness that we might learn of love. Now, draw us homeward once again to you, where we shall celebrate connections to each other and to you. Amen.

—*John C. Morgan*

TELLING THE OLD, OLD STORY

Help me, good and gracious God, to read, tell, and make alive the stories of the Bible for children. We live in a time when children know more about sitcoms and *Star Wars* than about David and Stephen. Prod me, O Lord, out of my shyness and lethargy, to read and to tell Bible

stories. May they find excitement and adventure in the stories of the Bible, and especially may they find grace and strength from the stories of Jesus. Amen.

RESPECTING ALL GENERATIONS

Gracious Parent, you are no respecter of persons, for your love makes persons of every age valuable and cherished. Although there are differences in generations, help us to value those differences, realizing we learn from each other. Help us, loving God, to respect and honor
>*the loyalty and sacrifice of the Civics;
>*the quiet presence and soft answers of the Silent Generation;
>*the integrity and concern for justice of the Boomers;
>*the commitment to family values of the GenXers;
>*the bright promise and dreams of the Millennials.

As we begin a new millennium, may this century bring all generations together in love and respect for one another other. Amen.

GIVE ME A SENSE OF DIRECTION, LORD

Lord, help me not to do for my children what they can do for themselves.

Help me not to offer them hand-outs when they can earn their own way.

Help me not to make up for what I missed by overloading them with things.

Help me to not offer advice when they can make their own decisions.

Help me to be responsible and to take charge of my life, so that they will take charge of theirs.

Amen.

I WANT TO BE THE WOMAN

He taught himself Greek
    at eighty years old
    because he'd always wanted to learn.

God,
I want to be like that!

I want to be the woman
   taking the course
   with the half-century start
    on her classmates.

I want to be the woman
   who cherishes the secret
   she's discovered
   that once you're old enough

you can get away with
wearing tennis shoes
anywhere
and with anything.

I want to be the woman
who's always hopeful enough
to plant another batch of bulbs
in the fall.

I want to be the woman
who always finds herself among
teachers,
some of whom are children
and teenagers.

I want to be the woman
who knows
that there's always
some new place to discover
up the road,
across the ocean,
in my heart.

I want to be the woman
who, for her 106th birthday
wanted to go dancing—
and did.

God,
Surely such people make you smile.
I want to be like that.

—*Peggy Haymes*

TEACH US

Father in heaven who lovest all,
O help Thy children when they call;
That they may build from age to age
An undefiled heritage.

Teach us to rule ourselves alway,
Controlled and cleanly night and day;
That we may bring, if need arise
No maimed or worthless sacrifice.

Teach us the strength that cannot seek,
By deed or thought, to hurt the weak:
That, under Thee, we may possess
Man's strength to comfort man's distress.

Teach us delight in simple things,
And mirth that has no bitter springs;
Forgiveness free of evil done,
And Love to all men 'neath the sun!

—*Rudyard Kipling, 1865–1936*

A CRY FOR JUSTICE . . . AND COMPASSION

Dear Lord, it seems as if old people can be very selfish, and only concerned with our own entitlements and preoccupied with our own pleasure and pursuits. Where there are injustices, and the old mistreated or exploited, we need to right those wrongs, and help in the name of charity. But we need a higher vision that makes us realize we are advocates for the underrepresented future generations.

Forgive us for idling away our days playing golf and taking cruises, or amusing ourselves until death. Grant that we may be deeply concerned about the world we leave our grandchildren and great-grandchildren, realizing that the real test of any generation is the kind of future we create for those who follow us.

May we plant trees under which we will never sit, and build bridges over which we will never cross. Amen

VI.

FACING LOSS AND DEATH

The cords of death entangled me,
the anguish of the grave came upon me;
I was overcome by trouble and sorrow.
Then I called on the name of the LORD:
"O LORD, save me!"

—Psalm 116:3-4, NIV

ON LEAVING MY HOME

Well, God, the time has come. I dreaded it so much, but it is time to leave my home. How I loved this place, and knew every nook and corner. A whole past unravels as we sort out old papers and scrapbooks. Events long past take on a new perspective, as if we were reliving them for the first time. I look around and see so much of my self lived here; the laughter of children and tears of sorrow have filled all these rooms, and now I must say good-bye. But I know it is better to let it go; and there is a sense of fulfillment, of having experienced life to its deepest in this place. Yet the truth remains: When we do not hold back from loss, it can be a new beginning. I hope I can remember this when the day of my death arrives. Amen.

ON MOVING TO A RETIREMENT COMMUNITY

Well, Lord, the day has come. In many ways I dreaded leaving my home, my security, And now I have to give up some of my privacy and live with other old people. Help me even now to accept these people as I find them—boring at times, stimulating, and garrulous. Help me remember that all these strange people are loved by you. Deliver me from being snappy at meals with people who are cranky—they may be in pain. If someone wants to confide a problem, help me listen. And may I reach out to those

when I feel the urge to strike out. As I leave my home, give me a sense of call, even as you called old Abraham and Sarah when they left their home on a new journey of faith. If I can love my neighbor there, then I have a mission. Amen.

WHEN I REMEMBER

In quiet moments before sleep and during the
    day
I remember the friends I've seen fall
Like withered leaves in autumn.
It makes me feel alone,
Like one who walks empty beaches
after the crowds have gone;
Like one who strides college streets
when students are on holiday,
and there is an eerie quiet.
No way can I forget my friends,
Whose presence brought treasured moments
    that still bring joy.
Amen.

NOW YOU ARE GONE

My child, you have toiled through life and come to the end of suffering: and now our lord has obliged you.

Now you have gone, gone to whatever kind of place it may be, the place where all are shorn, the place we all go to, the place of no lights and

no windows, never again to return, to come back. You will think no more of what lies here, of what lies behind you.

At the end of many days you went away and left your children, your grandchildren; you left them orphaned, you left them living. You will think no more of what may become of them.

We will go and join you, we will go be with you at the end of many days. Amen.

—*Aztec Prayer*

HOW SHORT LIFE IS

Eternal God, teach us to realize how very short life is, even if science may have helped us live longer than our parents. The marvels of technology have lengthened our days, but cannot tell us what this extra time means. A friend gets the death sentence of cancer; a child is snatched away by a senseless accident; a loved one has cardiac arrest and dies. We know how vulnerable to death our bodies are, how soon death comes. Help us to treasure each day as if it were our last. Like the sudden flash of lightning in the summer sky, remind us that every day our soul is required of us. So may we realize the preciousness of the moment, and that the greatest tragedy is not death, but what dies within us while we live. Amen.

ON WONDERING WHERE THEY ARE

Loving God, you alone understand how I often think about my loved ones who have left this earth. If only it were possible for one short hour for them to tell me what and where they are. But the gates guard their secrets well. When we are faced with the death of a loved one, all the arguments go out the window. When all's said and done, it remains a mystery. Where have they gone? How do they spend eternity? Will I ever see them again? Do they know my life now? This I know: if life ends in death, there is no final justice. This I know: as the first disciples saw Christ after his death, so I will know my loved ones in that land beyond the distant stars. Amen.

HOW BRIEF LIFE IS

Alpha and Omega, we like to think that we will live forever, and so we waltz through days and nights oblivious to our date with death. Our lives are really a puff of smoke, a blip on the computer screen, or like snow upon the river, a moment white, then gone forever. But then a phone call in the middle of the night; an accident on a rain slickened road; a funeral procession making its way to the cemetery, and we are reminded that life is short at best and there are no guarantees. Help us to cherish each day as if it were our last, and be kind to everyone

we meet. Through the one who lived and died and rose again, Jesus Christ. Amen.

GOD OF THE LIVING

I should like to remember my dead to you, O Lord, all those who once belonged to me and now have left me. There are many of them, far too many to be taken in one glance. If I am to pay my sad greetings to them all, I must travel back in memory over the entire route of my life's long journey.

When I look back in this way, I see my life as a long highway filled by a column of marching men. Every moment someone breaks out of the line and goes off silently, without a word or wave of farewell, to be swiftly enwrapped in the darkness of the night stretching out on both sides of the road. The number of marchers gets steadily smaller, for the new men coming up to fill the ranks are really not marching in my column at all. . . .

A strange thing happens to the man who really loves, for even before his own death his life becomes a life with the dead. Could a true lover ever forget his dead? When one has really loved, his forgetting is only apparent; he only *seems* to get over his grief. The quiet and composure he gradually regains are not a sign that things are as they were before, but a proof that his grief is ultimate and definitive. It shows that a piece of his own heart has really died and is now with the

living dead. This is the real reason he can weep no more. . . .

When I pray, "Grant them eternal rest, O Lord, and let Thy perpetual light shine upon them," let my words be only the echo of the prayer of love that they themselves are speaking for me in the silence of eternity. "O Lord, grant unto him, whom we love in Your Love now as never before, grant unto him after his life's struggle Your eternal rest, and let Your perpetual light shine also upon him, as it does upon us." Amen.

—Karl Rahner, 1904–1984

LAMENT IN A TIME OF GRIEF

Lord of the brokenhearted, you wept openly at the grave of your friend Lazarus, showing us once and for all that in every pain that rends the heart you have a part. We grieve the loss of our parents, spouses, and friends who have gone on that final journey that we all shall face one day. We know time does not heal our wounds, but makes them deeper. Bind up our wounds as we remember the wounds of Christ. Make sacred the memories of those whom we have loved long since and lost awhile. Teach us to live in this world with kindness, where we only see dimly as in a mirror, until we join our loved ones who now see face to face. Then we shall understand,

even as we are fully understood. Through the Wounded Healer, Jesus Christ. Amen.

PRAYER FOR GRACE

Lord, she just died a few hours ago, dear Grace, and they are already cleaning out her room in the nursing home. I stood there in reverent silence as they stuffed her belongings into a plastic bag and snuffed out her last mementos. How I miss her. She brought so much goodness and laughter despite being ninety-two years old. She turned a drab, dark nursing home room into a sanctuary of light with her quips and sense of humor. Her spirit never faltered even at the end, as she fought the good fight, kept the faith, and finished the course. She left us all a legacy of what it means to grow old *with grace*. Thank you for her life, dear Lord. They can try to extinguish all traces of that light, but the light of her life shines on in the darkness, and the darkness cannot put it out. Good-bye, dear friend. Your days on this earth were good and long, but your best days have just begun. Amen.

AT MY FUNERAL

Compassionate Friend, sitting in that small church I listened to the music of "For all the saints . . . " and thought about my funeral. The woman who had died was ninety-seven. Only a

few friends gathered, but her family filled six pews. I wonder who will come to my funeral. I am blessed with a large family, so I take comfort that they will be there. But down deep I know that what matters is not the attendance at my funeral but how I will be remembered after I am gone. How will I be remembered? And, for how long? Yet, what really matters is not how I am remembered, but the fact that you, God, remembered me through your gift of life in Christ. The timeless prayer for mercy of the dying thief is my prayer, too: "Jesus, remember me . . . " (Luke 23:42). And you will. Amen.

AT THE GRAVE

Oh God, we stand in silence at the grave, waiting for the words of committal. The tent poles are clanging in the winter wind, the family hushed and still, and all eyes are fixed on a casket. We wonder where she has gone and when it will be our turn. Lord, every day we should stand at the grave, for that day comes for all for whom it has been appointed once to die, and yet we try to block it out with every diversion conceivable to the mind. We don't want to be morbid, but we need to know that unless we rendezvous with death, we will never live fully. Help us to keep our hearts fixed on the one eternal empty tomb. Amen.

SOMETHING AWESOME BEYOND

Christ of Gethsemane, as I grow older every day I read obituaries of friends who have died, some younger than I. It is only by your mercy I have been spared to live out more days on this pilgrimage we call life. My life is torn by losses— some expected, some as unexpected as a thief in the night. These deaths make me aware of that final moment. I fear dying, and take comfort that Jesus himself faced death with anguish and pain in the garden. I can never fully grasp that struggle, and yet it brings peace that Christ knew my human fear. I have no idea of what lies beyond— it is beyond my comprehension—but I believe it must be so wonderful and awesome that it cannot be contained in any language. Death one day will be swallowed up in victory. Hallelujah! Amen.

FOR THE LIFE EVERLASTING

Bring us, O Lord God, at our last awakening into the house and gate of heaven, to enter into that gate and dwell in that house, where there shall be no darkness nor dazzling, but one equal light; no noise nor silence, but one equal music; no fears nor hopes, but one equal possession; no ends nor beginnings, but one equal eternity; in the habitations of your glory and dominion, world without end. Amen.

—John Donne, 1572–1631

AN OLD LIBRARY BOOK

Loving God, my friend has died. He often told me that he thought of his life as a library book. It was checked out years ago, but finally its spine is cracked and its edges have frayed. The book of his life was well read, but long overdue. It is a book we can all read and pass on to others. But the Head Librarian has called that book in. Amen.

AT MY PARENTS' GRAVES

I stood that cold afternoon and stared at my parents' graves. Often parted in this life by distance, now they lay side by side in that frozen ground. Inscribed on the gray stones were the dates of each one's birth and death. But what really mattered was that dash (–), the years in between. For me this became a moment of truth, Lord, as I realized that the sands of the hourglass are getting near the bottom, and one day everyone will return from the cemetery except me! What will my children and grandchildren be thinking as they stand at my grave on that day? I wonder. Amen.

LAST WORDS

Dear God, I think of the final words of Gandhi as he was assassinated, "O God" and then this great person of history left this world. I remember today three good friends who have died and gone to be with you. I spoke with Bob just a few days ago outside the city bank. He had a massive coronary and died on a hiking trail in the pristine world he loved so well. I remember John. On his way to baptize a dying child he suffered a stroke, drove through a stop sign, and died in a shattering of glass. And Wade, age eighty-one, vibrant to the end. He died on the tennis court after a smashing serve. None of my friends died in the usual manner—slipping away at home or in a hospital room, or gasping for that final breath in a nursing home. I remember now how my father preached a sermon from Micah 6:8 called "Have a Good Day," then died in his sleep. All died in good faith and, like Gandhi, cried, "O God." Amen.

THE PRAYER OF ST. RICHARD
AS HE LAY DYING

Thanks be to thee,
Lord Jesus Christ,
for all the benefits
which thou hast won for us,
for all the pains and insults
which thou hast borne for us.
O most merciful Redeemer,
Friend and Brother,
may we know thee more clearly,
and follow thee more nearly,
day by day.

—Bishop Richard Chichester, 1197–1253

GRIEF

For most of us death appears as a fixed horizon, and those who pass over it leave an emptiness we must fill with a season of grieving. And yet, with our sorrow there is also a knowledge of light, a certainty that the sense of loss belongs not to any ending but to the limitations of our vision. Death is an experience for those left behind, not for those who are moving from one stage of living to another. It is the Christ who dwells within us who is free to step back and forth over the horizon of death. Christ contains our grief in his passion and our knowledge of light in his transcendence. He shows us that

death and resurrection are the two sides of the
one coin.

WHEN A SPOUSE DIES

O God, she is dead; she is gone,
the best friend I ever had.
My world is empty. Nothing matters.
I find no joy in anything, and wish I could die
    myself.

Everywhere I turn I see her,
and up come my tears again.
My nights are restless, long,
and all my days are grey.
The ache inside is huge, gaping,
the only thing I feel.

I was not a perfect husband, God. You know that.
How sorry it makes me now.
Why couldn't I see how good and precious she was?
I would have curbed the sharp word
and let the little things go.
I would have told her and showed her more often
    how
much I loved her.

God, I don't know what to do.
There seems nothing left for me.
I am a burden to myself and no good to anyone.

Jesus, Healer of Souls, I need you as never before.
Reach down to me and pull me to my feet.

Call me from the tomb. Breathe on me that I
may live.

—Kathleen Fischer and Thomas Hart

DEATH IS ONLY A HORIZON

We give back to you, O God, those whom you
gave to us. You did not lose them when you gave
them to us, and we do not lose them by their
return to you. Your dear Son has taught us that
life is eternal and love cannot die. So death is
only an horizon and an horizon is only the limit
of our sight. Open our eyes to see more clearly,
and draw us closer to you so that we may know
that we are nearer to our loved ones who are
with you. You have told us that you are
preparing a place for us. Prepare us also for that
happy place, that where you are we may also be
always, O dear Lord of life and death.

—William Penn, 1644–1718

A GLIMPSE OF HEAVEN

Dear Lord and Father of us all, you have set eternity in our hearts; we know that this life cannot
ultimately satisfy us, we yearn for a better world.
We look forward to that place Jesus called
"heaven." There our old parents hold each other
in youthful bodies with a love that never ends.

There our children are always in our arms, and we see friends whose presence we have missed all these years. And, by your grace, we touch those who have touched history as we merge with saints and angels. Lord, we believe; help our unbelief. Amen.

AT THE DEATH OF A LOVED ONE

Dear Loving Lord, I come to you in deep sorrow because my loved one (parent, child, spouse) has died. I know that it is good for me to grieve, and that your grace will ease my pain. Help me to forgive the wrongs I have done to _____. Have mercy on _____, and let us be reunited one day in your eternal home. Amen.

GIVE ME, GOOD LORD

Glorious God, give me grace to amend my life, and to have an eye to my end without begrudging death, which to those who die in you, good Lord, is the gate of a wealthy life.

And give me, good Lord, a humble, lowly, quiet, peaceable, patient, charitable, kind, tender and pitiful mind, in all my works and all my words and all my thoughts, to have a taste of your holy, blessed Spirit.

Give me, good Lord, a full faith, a firm hope, and a fervent charity, a love of you incomparably above the love of myself.

Give me, good Lord, a longing to be with you, not to avoid the calamities of this world, nor so much to attain the joys of heaven, as simply for love of you.

And give me, good Lord, your love and favour, which my love of you, however great it might be, could not deserve were it not for your great goodness.

These things, good Lord, that I pray for, give me your grace to labour for.

—Thomas More, 1478–1535
(written a week before his execution)

ON SAYING GOOD-BYE TO AN OLD FRIEND

Light of our darkness, I walked slowly down that endless hall of the nursing home with a heavy heart. I heard old John call out to me as I drifted into the present, "Missed you; wish you were back." He had dwindled down to almost skin and bones, and yet his spirit remained strong. We had had many laughs together, shared stories, and heard each other's heartaches. Now he was trying to say good-bye. How hard it is to say good-bye. You knew that, dear God, when Jesus said good-bye to his friends and left them his peace. Help John to bear his cross. Help me to be there for him in these final weeks or days. May I hear that willowy voice calling after me. Grant John the final victory that comes to all who love you. Amen.

PRAYER FOR DEATH ROW

God of ages, we enter death row when we realize that life is terminal and we don't have time to do all the things we planned. Death's door seems far away, but then we know there is a date set for us on death row. What will we find behind that door? Some are terribly afraid; others not sure. Help us to remember what Jesus taught us: The eleventh-hour worker gets the full pay. Grace will prevail. Amen.

GIVING PERMISSION TO DIE

Lord of life, one of the gifts we can give our family and friends is allowing them to die well. We cling to them, even in their dying hours, and have a hard time letting them go. I sat with Grace and Mildred as they gave that permission to Olin. Tired and worn out, he struggled against death, but they told him, "It's okay, Daddy, to let go. We love you. God loves you. It's time to go home." Olin sighed and breathed his last. I remembered Jesus' last words from the cross, a prayer he learned from the psalms, *"Father, into your hands I commend my spirit"* (Luke 23:46). Grant that all of us die with that prayer in our hearts. Amen.

HOW PAINFUL IT IS

When we lose a loved one, we are left with a grief that never goes away. For a while, it disappears in the routine of life, but then it returns like waves rolling over us. When Christmas, a birthday, Thanksgiving, or an anniversary comes we remember and feel deeply the loved one's absence and the hole in our existence. So we go through the cycles again—denial, anger, bargaining, depression—until finally we let them go and reach some acceptance. Amen.

PREPARED

Life teaches us that death can come like a thief in the night. Just when we least expect it death comes. A shattering car accident, a sudden coronary, a fatal light, a flood can snatch loved ones and us from this life. How can we be prepared, O God, to die? Not by endless, morbid preoccupation with death, but with living well and not having any unfinished relational business. When we are ready to die at any moment, we are also prepared to live fully. Amen.

AT LAST

When on my day of life the night is
    falling,
  And, in the winds from unsunned
    spaces blown,
I hear far voices out of darkness call-
    ing
  My feet to paths unknown,

Thou who hast made my home of life
    so pleasant,
  Leave not its tenant when its walls
    decay;
O Love Divine, O Helper ever present,
  Be Thou my strength and stay!

Be near me when all else from me
    drifting:
  Earth, sky, home's pictures, days
    of shade and shine,
And kindly faces to my own uplifting
  The love which answers mine.

I have but Thee, my Father! let Thy
    spirit
  Be with me then to comfort and
    uphold;
No gate of pearl, no branch of palm
    I merit,
  Nor street of shining gold.

Suffice it if—my good and ill un-

reckoned,
   And both forgiven through Thy
      abounding grace—
I find myself by hands familiar beck-
      oned
   Unto my fitting place.

Some humble door among Thy many
      mansions,
   Some sheltering shade where sin
      and striving cease,
And flows for ever through heaven's
      green expansions
   The river of Thy peace.

There, from the music round about
      me stealing,
   I fain would learn the new and
      holy song,
And find at last, beneath Thy trees
      of healing,
   The life for which I long.

   —John Greenleaf Whittier, 1807–1892

VII.

REDEEMING SUFFERING

*So we do not lose heart. Even though our outer
nature is wasting away, our inner nature is
being renewed day by day.
For this slight momentary affliction
is preparing us for an eternal weight
of glory.*

—2 Corinthians 4:16-17

HELP ME RISE ABOVE MY BODY

O Spirit of God, you breathed life into a formless void and made this beautiful world; even in our old bodies you dwell as light in darkness. Forgive me for being so preoccupied with my body and obsessed with my health. I know I am more than my body, but I can't help worrying about my body now. I don't see or hear as well as I used to, and my joints ache with arthritis. Your mercy has spared me serious illness, and yet every day I struggle with my body. Help me to rise above this, and realize that my body is just a tent I live in, and someday it will not be subject to pain, aging, or death. It is getting late, and the shadows flit across my life. Some day it will be eternal light. There I will never be bogged down by my body or distracted. In that hope I live each day. I believe with all my heart you will change this earthly body to become a glorified new body. Amen.

IN SERIOUS SICKNESS

Lord Jesus Christ, you are the only source of health for the living, and you promise eternal life to the dying. I entrust myself to your holy will. If you wish me to stay longer in this world, I pray that you will heal me of my present sickness. If you wish me to leave this world, I readily lay aside this mortal body, in the sure hope of receiving an immortal body which shall enjoy

everlasting health. I only ask that you relieve me of pain, that whether I live or die, I may rest peaceful and contented.

—Erasmus, 1466–1536

HELP ME NOT TO COMPLAIN

So often I complain, dear Lord, about my little ailments and inconveniences. I whine and give organ recitals to all my friends. Help me to lift my eyes to the cross of Jesus, where he felt the anguish of everyone and bore the whole human tragedy in his spirit. May I realize that we will not be spared suffering, but there can be a strength given by you to help us bear it. I need your help. Help me transcend these problems by contemplating your pain. Help us to let go and dance within the storm. Amen.

FORGIVING MYSELF

God of all mercy, you who always pardon all who ask, help me as I try to forgive myself. I realize, my Lord, that unless I can forgive myself I cannot fully forgive those who have offended me. I forgive myself for being too impatient, especially when it takes so long to heal. I forgive myself for my foolish words, for being too quick to speak, for not taking time to think. I forgive myself for blaming others for my faults, for

finding scapegoats that take me off the hook. I forgive myself for those small sins of older age: whining and complaining, being irritable and grouchy, and my narrowness of mind and heart. Help me to receive your forgiveness and accept your grace. Amen.

WHY, LORD?

Lord, suffering disturbs me, oppresses me. I don't understand why you allow it. Why, Lord? Why this dear old man, who has been dying for months, is kept alive because of modern medicine? Why this woman, languishing in a nursing home, is lying in bed with that awful blank look? Why this husband with Alzheimer's is visited every day by his wife even though he doesn't know her? Why this lovely lady dying with cancer seems ten years older than she is? Why, Why, Why? Why this hideous suffering falls unfairly on good people and spares evil people? Why can't science find cures for these diseases? I don't understand!

SIOUX PRAYER

O our Father, the Sky, hear us
    and make us strong.
O our Mother the Earth, hear us
    and give us support.
O Spirit of the East,

send us your Wisdom.
O Spirit of the South,
   may we tread your path of life.
O Spirit of the West,
   may we always be ready for the long
journey.
O Spirit of the North, purify us
   with your cleansing winds.

—Sioux prayer

IN YOUR MIDST

I, God, am in your midst.
Whoever knows me can never fall,
   Not in the heights,
   Nor in the depths,
   Nor in the breadths,
   For I am love,
Which the vast expanse of evil
   Can never still.

—Hildegard of Bingen, 1098–1179

DURING A SERIOUS ILLNESS

Dear Lord, you suffered so much pain in order to save me and all mankind from sin. Yet I feel it hard to bear even this little pain in my body. Lord, because of your great pain, have mercy on my little pain. And if you wish me simply to bear

the pain, send me the patience and the courage which I lack. It may seem strange to say it, but I would rather suffer the spiritual pain from the insults people hurl against me, in place of this physical pain. Indeed I enjoy spiritual pain suffered for your sake; and I happily embrace the disrespect of this world, so long as I am obeying your will. But in my feebleness, I cannot endure this present illness. Save me from it.

—Margery Kempe, c. 1373–1438

THE ONE THING NECESSARY

Lord, you gave me health and I forgot you.
You take it away and I come back to you.
What infinite compassion that God, in order to
give himself to me,
takes away his gifts which I allowed to come
between me and him.
Lord, take away everything that is not you.
All is yours.
You are the Lord.
Dispose everything, comforts, success, health.
Take all the things that possess me instead of
you
that I may be wholly yours.

—François Fénelon, 1651–1715

THE SIXTEENTH PSALM

Lord, the Bible is the book I always come back to. In these retirement years it speaks again and again in new and exciting ways. Why, just today I felt downcast and anxious, preoccupied with my body, and some of the problems of old age. Then I meditated on the sixteenth psalm, and it was a light breaking into my darkness. *"Protect me, O God, for in you I take refuge"* (Ps. 16:1). Yes, dear God, preserve me from the evil days when I take no pleasure in them, when all I think about are my ailments and fears. I will try and allow these words to direct this day and rule over this night: *"I keep the Lord always before me; because he is at my right hand, I shall not be moved"* (Ps. 16:8). Lead me beyond all these fears to faith, save me from catastrophizing that every symptom is a sign of disease, and give me the peace that only comes when you are at my right hand. Amen.

PSALM 13

How long will the pain go on, Lord,
  this grief I can hardly bear?
How long will anguish grip me
  and agony wring my mind?
Light up my eyes with your presence;
  let me feel your love in my bones.
Keep me from losing myself
  in ignorance and despair.
Teach me to be patient, Lord;

teach me to be endlessly patient.
Let me trust that your love enfolds me
  when my heart feels desolate and dry.
I will sing to the Lord at all times,
  even from the depths of pain.

—trans. Stephen Mitchell

PSALM 4

Even in the midst of great pain, Lord,
  I will praise you for what is.
I will not refuse this grief
  or close myself to anguish.
Let shallow men pray for ease:
  "Comfort us, shield us from sorrow."
I pray for whatever you send me,
  and I ask to receive it as your gift.
You have put a joy in my heart
  greater than all the world's riches.
I lie down trusting the darkness,
  for I know that even now you are here.

—trans. Stephen Mitchell

RESPECT LIFE'S HARD TIMES

It is the wind and the rain, O God, the cold and
the storm that make this earth of Thine to
blossom and bear its fruit. So in our lives it is
storm and stress and hurt and suffering that

make real men and women bring the world's work to its highest perfection. Let us learn then in these growing years to respect the harder sterner aspects of life together with its joy and laughter, and to weave them all into the great web which hangs holy to the Lord. Amen

—*W. E. B. Du Bois, 1868–1963*

IN A TIME OF DESPAIR

Light of our darkness, how can I forget that night when I drove home alone with darkness as my only companion and faced the specters of the mind. I was waiting for the results of a biopsy that would reveal whether or not I had cancer. I felt a godforsaken loneliness that consumed me. I wept as I drove through that eerie night. Then I believe you sent me the words of a hymn that buoyed my spirits and gave me hope:

> Lead, kindly Light, amid the encircling gloom, Lead thou me on;
> The night is dark, and I am far from home; Lead thou me on.
> Keep thou my feet; I do not ask to see The distant scene; one step enough for me.

It was an Emmaus Road moment. Despair gave way to hope. It was as if the Stranger of Nazareth rode with me. Thanks be to God. Amen.

THE DEEP BEAUTY OF AUTUMN

Master Painter,
as the days grow short
  and the chill winds blow
you color the trees more beautifully every day,
  brushing the leaves with brilliant hues
  of reds and golds until
  suddenly
  and quietly
  they fall.

And our lives should be like that, too,
  I think,
for, as the days grow short
  and the bones begin to chill,
you color our days with the brilliant hues
  of experience and wisdom,
but we—
  we miss the beauty and see only the fall,
for, by worshipping the fleeting youth of spring
  we have become blinded to the deep beauty
   of autumn!

—*Mary Sue H. Rosenberger*

WHAT GOOD SUFFERING DOES

God of all comfort, help me to see the benefits of suffering. It is the one time in life when we are thrown back on our own resources. It tests our ability to wait, to tolerate the unknown, and to

find inner strength. So suffering does mold character. Help us also to know that good eventually comes out of everything. Through suffering we meet new people, discover new beginnings, and find a resilience of heart to continue our journey. May we truly believe it is the obstacles that we have to transcend in life that bring out the best in us. Amen.

A PSALM

O God, I have cried unto you.
My whole being has sought you out.
O God, I have wrestled with you;
In my pain I cry to you for help.
In my weakness, I seek your strength.
If I cry out, will you hear me?
If I weep, will you dry my tears?
Be like a mother to me; gather me in your
    arms.
Be like a father to me; protect me from evil.
Our days, they seem as deepening shadows
Casting darkness on the land.
Our moments, like grass, wither in the sun.
Send light, O God, and let us live!
Send light, O God, and let us live!
No creature lives but that she dies;
No flower blooms nor tree nor plant but that
    they end.
O God, we do not ask for more than these:
The strength to bear the pain,
Your presence in the evening star,

Glad praise when day is done.
Praise Life that in us grows,
For time and toil and love,
For every moment of our days,
For what we are is yours.

—*John C. Morgan*

REMEMBERING THE FRAIL ELDERLY

Jesus said, "The poor you will always have with you." This prayer of W. E. B. Du Bois reminds us that we always have the frail elderly with us, and our prayers need to be with them.

Remember with us tonight, O God, the old and helpless—those who have reached length of days and know life with its joys and bitterness and have come in the evening to the long shadows, unloved and uncared for and alone. May we in our youth and gladness and plenty never forget these silent sentinels of pain and neglect who stand to warn us against extravagance and undutifulness and careless ease. Someone has forgotten his duty toward each of these pitiful souls. May we never forget our duty which Thy voice sounded from Sinai: Honor thy father and thy mother that their days may be long in the Land. Amen.

—*W. E. B. Du Bois, 1868–1963*

WHEN TRAGEDY STRIKES

Healer of persons, we find it hard to believe you are really in control when tragedy touches our lives. We know you have not made it happen, but you have allowed it. There is the tragedy of those who know their lives will be short. We marvel at their courage, and realize that we could not find such grace if it happened to us. We find in their patience and gentleness the spirit of Christ.

There is the tragedy of those who live too long. They linger and languish, wanting to go to their heavenly home, but remain in pain on this earth. Help them to be patient and to find you in the love that surrounds them

There is the tragedy of those who have lost loved ones. We easily feel that if you have been there it would not have happened. But you were there, even as you were present in the death of your Son. Grant that those who mourn may pick up the threads of their lives again.

There is the tragedy of those who have caused pain in the lives of others through abuse or neglect or harmful actions. Help them to find forgiveness. In all our afflictions help us to turn to the One who bore our sufferings and carried our griefs. We do not understand, but you do. Amen.

MOST RICHLY BLESSED
(Prayer of an Unknown Confederate Soldier)

I asked God for strength, that I might achieve,
I was made weak, that I might learn
    humbly to obey . . .
I asked for health, that I might do greater
    things,
I was given infirmity, that I might do better
    things . . .
I asked for riches, that I might be happy,
I was given poverty, that I might be wise . . .
I asked for power, that I might have praise of
    men,
I was given weakness, that I might feel the
    need of God . . .
I asked for all things, that I might enjoy life,
I was given life, that I might enjoy all things . . .
I got nothing that I asked for but everything
    that I had hoped for.
Almost despite myself, my unspoiled prayers
    were answered.
I am among all men most richly blessed.

—Author Unknown

PRAYER OF A FRAIL ELDER

Lord, I thank you that in your love you have taken from me all earthly riches, and that you now clothe and feed me through the kindness of others. Lord, I thank you, that since you have

taken from me the sight of my eyes, you serve me now with the eyes of others.

Lord, I thank you that since you have taken away the power of my hands and my heart, you serve me by the hands and hearts of others. Lord, I pray for them. Reward them for it in your heavenly love, that they may faithfully serve and please you till they reach a happy end.

—*Mechtilde of Magdeburg, 1210–1285*

HELP HER TO REDISCOVER HER PAST, LORD

My friend has Alzheimer's disease, Lord. Some illnesses deprive people only of the present time, as they lose a piece of time when they are sick before recovery. Others who suffer from terminal illness lose hope for their future as they battle against death. But my friend has lost her past, as all memory of prior events, relationships, and persons slips away. Gracious God, there are moments when she does recall and repeats old stories in her garbled language. It is hard to sift through her broken sentences. I strain to grasp the meaning of her jumbled words. Help me to be there for her, Lord, for I may be the very instrument of your grace as I give her the gift of listening, even recording her stories. Amen.

A GIFT SHE GIVES

Thank you, Lord, for the gift that Mary gives us from her wheelchair. She gives to us a smile, a look, or a cheerful word. But her greatest gift is letting us serve her. We know it is more blessed to give than to receive, but it is blessed to receive, too, for it makes those who give feel they make a difference and are important. It was only when Peter allowed Jesus to wash his feet, and received that gift, that Peter understood the kingdom. Amen.

PRAYER FOR SUFFERERS

Loving God of the journey, I struggle as I face limits and lose dreams. I grapple with the broken relationships in my life. I weep as I confront lost dreams.

Be with me in my suffering, Lord; transform it with Your grace. Remind me that Your way is the way of strength in weakness, power in powerlessness, and life in death.

Remind me that I need not suffer alone. Send me those who will show me Your saving love in their presence.

Help me to seek You in the mystery and the journey. Remind me to look for the Yes's in Your No's to me.

—*Juliana Cooper-Goldenberg*

PRAYING THROUGH CHRONIC PAIN

Lord God, I do not pray for this pain to leave. I've prayed that prayer a thousand times, and I confess I was terribly angry at you for not healing my affliction. I know now the thorn will remain in my flesh, and I might as well get used to it. Forgive those who can't understand how I feel, because my pain is too hidden to be understood and I don't wear my heart on my sleeve. But between you and me, dear God, I have to know if there is meaning in this persistent pain. Will your grace really be sufficient? Can I find strength in weakness? Amen.

SCARS

I don't know exactly what you looked like, Jesus of Nazareth, when you walked the dusty roads of Galilee. I have seen many faded pictures, but none captures your face. You belong to every person, and something of us all lies hidden in your face. But I see the scars in your hands, made permanent by the hammers of soldiers. Those scars remind me of who you are. My little scars can hardly be mentioned in the same breath, and yet they tell me who I am. Not just the scars from childhood accidents or football games, but the scars on the soul. They remind me of the pain and anguish I've known on this earth. Most of my scars are my own doing—stupid mistakes, careless blunders. I wish I could

say I had more scars that are marks of the Lord Jesus. But thanks be to God your scars cover mine. Amen.

IT'S SO SAD, LORD

She sits glued to her comfortable chair. She understands God and refuses to go anywhere. Her husband is in the hospital and the doctor says he can't go home again. There is panic in her children's eyes as they beg her to go to Assisted Living, but she refuses. "Lived here for forty-five years, and don't expect to leave now," she mutters. They plead. She doesn't seem to hear. They argue. She smiles. They try to reason with her, and she dismisses their words with a shrug. "I can take care of him here," she says. "Been doing it for years." It's so sad, Lord. But there is no other way. They have to leave their home. Give to her and her children extra grace to find the way through this impasse. Amen.

FRIENDS WHO STAND BY

God of grace, thank you for friends who are born for adversity; so that when troubles come we are not alone. We find our truest support from those who have been wounded by life and use their wounds to heal us. A minister whose daughter is in prison offers compassion to others who are disgraced. A retired man who has experienced

anxiety visits a severely depressed retiree. A daughter whose mother is consumed by cancer reaches out to others who suffer cancer. A young couple whose parents are in a nursing home befriend other residents. A wife whose husband has Alzheimer's helps to form a support group for other caregivers. Thank you, Lord, for those who stand by us in our pain. Amen.

WOUNDED HEALERS

We are all, to varying degrees, spiritual cripples, wounded before we could name the hurt, bruised without knowing why. Each of us carries a pervasive sense of sadness within, as if we had lost something precious.

We have.

To name and touch our own deep hurt is to understand ourselves as wounded, but also to feel connected to the wounds of others. Might not our feelings then be those of compassion and gentleness to others, with whom we share the same wounds?

It is not out of self-satisfaction that we are able to pray. We do not pray out of abundance— but need. We pray as losers because this describes who we are when the masks are down. And when we understand this truth even our wounds are gifts.

—*John C. Morgan*

EPILOGUE
*The prayer of Simeon when he held the baby Jesus
in his arms.*

Master, now you are dismissing
    your servant in peace,
    according to your word;
for my eyes have seen your salvation,
    which you have prepared in
    the presence of all peoples,
a light for revelation to the
    Gentiles
    and for glory to your people
    Israel.

—Luke 2:29-32

Jesus' last prayer from the cross
Father, into your hands I commend my spirit.

—Luke 23:46

THE BOOKMARK

Trust in God
Let nothing disturb you,
let nothing frighten you;
All things pass:
God never changes.
Patience achieves
all it strives for.

He who has God
finds he lacks nothing,
God alone suffices.

—Teresa of Avila, 1515–1582, her bookmark

LAST EARTHLY PRAYER

Care thou for mine whom I must leave behind;
Care that they know who 'tis for them takes
    care;
Thy present patience help them still to bear;
Lord, keep them clearing, growing, heart and
    mind;
In one thy oneness us together bind;
Last earthly prayer with which to thee I cling—
Grant that, save love, we owe not anything.

—George MacDonald, 1824–1905

FINAL PRAYER

O Lord, support us all the day long, until the
shadows lengthen and the evening comes, and
the busy world is hushed, and the fever of life is
over, and our work is done. Then in your mercy
grant us a safe lodging, and a holy rest, and
peace at the last.

—John Henry Newman, 1801–1890

INDEX

III. Accepting Our Aging

IV. Discerning the Meaning of Our Stories

V. Mentoring the Next Generations

VI. Facing Loss and Death

Index of Prayers by Author

Notes and Permissions

"Aztec Prayer for the Deceased," from *The Sacred Path* by John Bierhorst. Copyright © 1983 by John Bierhorst. Used by permission of Morrow Junior Books, a division of William Morrow & Co., Inc.

Basil of Caesarea, "The Ship of Life," from *Bedside Prayers*, June Cotner, comp. (New York: HarperCollins, 1997), 49.

Black Elk, "The Tree Has Never Bloomed," from *American Indian Poetry*, George W. Cronyn, ed. Copyright © 1918, renewed 1962 by George W. Cronyn. Reprinted by permission of Ballantine Books, a division of Random House, Inc.

John David Burton, "Amplius," from *Naked in the Street* (Bellevue, Wash.: Ontos, 1985), 8. Used by permission of the author.

John Calvin, from *The HarperCollins Book of Prayers*, Robert Van de Weyer, comp. (New York: HarperCollins, 1993), 79.

William Ellery Channing, "My Symphony," from *Bedside Prayers*, June Cotner, comp. (New York: HarperCollins Publishers, 1997), 79.

Juliana Cooper-Goldenberg, "Prayer for Sufferers." Used by permission of the author.

John Donne, "Preserve My Soul," from *The Book of Uncommon Prayer*, Constance Pollock and Daniel Pollock, eds. (Dallas: Word Publishing, 1996), 50; "For the Life Everlasting," from *The Communion of Saints*, Horton Davies, ed. (Grand Rapids, Mich.: William B. Eerdmans Publishing Co., 1990), 91.

W. E. B. Du Bois, from *Prayers for Dark People,* by W. E. B. Du Bois; Herbert Aptheker, ed. (Amherst, Mass.: The University of Massachusetts Press, 1980), 43, 46. Copyright © 1980 by The University of Massachusetts Press. Used by permission of the publisher.

Erasmus, "In Serious Illness," from *The HarperCollins Book of Prayers*, Robert Van de Weyer, comp. (New York: HarperCollins Publishers, 1993), 137.

François Fénelon, from *Autumn Wisdom*, James E. Miller, ed. (Minneapolis, Minn.: Augsburg Press, 1995), 34.

Kathleen Fischer and Thomas Hart, "When a Spouse Dies," from *A Counselor's Prayer Book* (New York: Paulist Press, 1994), 112. Copyright © 1994 by Kathleen Fischer and Thomas Hart. Used by permission of Paulist Press.

Joseph Folliet, "A Little Prayer," from *The Evening Sun* by Joseph Folliet; David Smith, trans. (Chicago: Franciscan Herald Press, 1983), 46–47. Copyright © 1983 by Franciscan Herald Press. Used by permission.

"For the Coming Generations," from *The Book of Common Prayer* (New York: The Oxford University Press, 1990), 829.

George Fox, from *The Communion of Saints*, Horton Davies, ed. (Grand Rapids, Mich.: William B. Eerdmans Publishing Co., 1990), 91.

Romano Guardini, from *Journey to the Light: Spirituality as We Mature*, Ann Finch, ed. (New York: New City Press, 1996), 124.

Peggy Haymes, "I Want to Be the Woman," from *Heart Prayers* (Macon, Ga: Peake Road, 1997), 4–5. Copyright © 1997 by Peggy Haymes. Used by permission of the author.

Hildegard of Bingen, from *Prayers for All People*, Mary Ford-Grabowsky, ed. (New York: Doubleday, 1995), 272.

Ignatius of Loyola, from *The United Methodist Hymnal* (Nashville, Tenn.: The United Methodist Publishing House, 1989), 570.

Kathy Keay, "Spinning Tops" and "Broken Friendships," from *Laughter, Silence and Shouting*, Kathy Keay, comp. (London: HarperCollins Publishers, 1994), 95, 63. Used by permission of HarperCollins Publishers, Ltd.

Margery Kempe, "During a Serious Illness," from *The HarperCollins Book of Prayers*, Robert Van de Weyer, comp. (New York: HarperCollins Publishers, 1993), 224.

Rudyard Kipling, "Teach Us," from *The Book of Uncommon Prayer*, Constance Pollock and Daniel Pollock, eds. (Dallas: Word Publishing, 1996), 100.

George MacDonald, from *The Diary of an Old Soul* (London: George Allen & Unwin, 1905), 13.

Mechtilde of Magdeburg, from *Prayers of the Saints*, Woodeene Koenig-Bricker, ed. (New York: HarperCollins Publishers, 1996), 80–81.

Beth Ann Miller, "Litany for Older Adult Week 1997," from *AGEnda* (Presbyterian Church USA). Used by permission of the author.

Thomas More, "Give Me, Good Lord," from *The Book of Uncommon Prayer*, Constance Pollock and Daniel Pollock, eds. (Dallas: Word Publishing, 1996), 111.

John C. Morgan, "The Pleas of a Lost Child." Used by permission of the author. "A Psalm" and "Wounded Healers" from *Prayerfulness: A Monthly Guide to Spirituality*, pp. 24, 56. Copyright © 1993 by John C. Morgan. Used by permission of the author.

"Native American Prayer," from *The United Methodist Hymnal* (Nashville, Tenn.: The United Methodist Publishing House, 1989), 329.

John Henry Newman, from *One Prayer at a Time*, F. Forrester Church and Terrence J. Mulry, eds. (New York, London: Macmillan Publishing Company, Collier Macmillan Publishers, 1989), 129.

The Peacemaker, from *Pearls of Wisdom from Grandma*, Jennifer Gates Hayes, ed. (New York: HarperCollins Publishers 1997), ix.

William Penn, from *The Communion of Saints*, Horton Davies, ed. (Grand Rapids, Mich.: William B. Eerdmans Publishing Co., 1990), 97.

"Prayer of an Aging Woman," from *Laughter, Silence and Shouting*, Kathy Keay, comp. (London: HarperCollins Publishers, 1994), 118. Used by permission of HarperCollins Publishers, Ltd.

"Prayer of an Unknown Confederate Soldier," from *Bedside Prayers*, June Cotner, ed. (New York: HarperCollins Publishers, 1997), 65.

"Prayer of the Third Age," from *Journey to the Light*, Ann Finch, ed. (London: New City Press, 1991), 123. Used by permission of New City London.

Psalms 13 and 4, from *A Book of Psalms*, Stephen Mitchell, trans. (New York: HarperCollins, 1993); 6, 4. Copyright © 1993 by Stephen Mitchell. Reprinted by permission of HarperCollins Publishers, Inc.

Karl Rahner, "God of the Living," from *Prayers for a Lifetime*, Albert Raffelt, ed. (New York: Crossroad Publishing Co., 1986), 144–145; 149. Copyright © The Crossroad Publishing Co. Used by permission of the publisher.

Richard of Chichester, from Eerdmans' *Book of Famous Prayers*, Veronica Zundel, comp. (Grand Rapids, Mich.: William B. Eerdmans Publishing Co., 1983), 31.

Kim Richardson, "A Teenager's Prayer Prayer," from *Dreams Alive: Prayers by Teenagers*, ed. by Carl Koch (Winona, Minn.: Saint Mary's Press, 1991), 48. Used by permission of the publisher. All rights reserved.

Mary Sue H. Rosenberger, "The Deep Beauty of Autumn," from *Sacraments in My Refrigerator*. Used by permission of the author.

Chief Seattle (attr.), from *Prayers for the Common Good*, A. Jean Lesher, ed. (Cleveland, Ohio: The Pilgrim Press, 1998), 134–135.

"Sioux Prayer," from *Prayers for Healing*, Maggie Oman, ed. (Berkeley, Ca.: Conari Press, 1997), 80.

Pierre Teilhard de Chardin, from *The Divine Milieu* (New York: Harper Colophon Books, 1960), 89–90. Copyright © 1957 by Editions du Seuill, Paris. English translation copyright © 1960 by Wm. Collins Sons & Co., London; and Harper & Row, Publishers, Inc., New York. Renewed © 1988 by Harper & Row Publishers, Inc. Reprinted by permission of HarperCollins Publishers, Inc.

Teresa of Avila, "A Busy, Frantic Life," from *The HarperCollins Book of Prayers*, Robert Van de Weyer, comp. (New York: HarperCollins Publishers, 1993), 348; "The Bookmark," from *The Complete Book of Christian Prayer* (New York: The Continuum Publishing Company, 1997), 460.

Thérèse of Lisieux, from *The Complete Book of Christian Prayer* (New York: The Continuum Publishing Company, 1995), 317.

Thomas à Kempis, "For Discernment," from Eerdmans' *Book of Famous Prayers*, Veronica Zundel, comp. (Grand Rapids, Mich.: William B. Eerdmans Publishing Co., 1983), 38; "A Saint's Prayer," from *Prayers from the Imitation of Christ*, Ronald Klug, ed. (Minneapolis, Minn: Augsburg Fortress, 1996), 79.

Charles Wesley, "O Thou Who Camest From Above," from *The United Methodist Hymnal* (Nashville, Tenn.: The United Methodist Publishing House, 1989), p. 501; "Everyone's Prayer from *The HarperCollins Book of Prayers*, Robert Van de Weyer, comp. (New York: HarperCollins Publishers, 1993), 383.

John Greenleaf Whittier, "Dear Lord and Father of Mankind," from *The United Methodist Hymnal* (Nashville, Tenn.: The United Methodist Publishing House, 1989), 358; "At Last," from The Poetical *Works of John Greenleaf Whittier* (Edinburgh: W.P. Nimmo, Hay, & Mitchell, n.d.), 523.

Ella Wheeler Wilcox, "Whatever Is—Is Best," from *Bedside Prayers*, June Cotner, comp. (New York: HarperCollins Publishers, 1997), 46–47.

Frederick Zydeck, "Praying for Stuff," from *The Christian Century* (July 16–23, 1997), 648. Copyright 1997 Christian Century Foundation. Reprinted by permission.